IN A HARBOUR GREEN

IN A HARBOUR GREEN

CELEBRATING BENEDICT KIELY

EDITED BY

GEORGE O'BRIEN

IRISH ACADEMIC PRESS

First published in 2019 by
Irish Academic Press
10 George's Street
Newbridge
Co. Kildare
Ireland
www.iap.ie

© George O'Brien; individual contributors 2019

9781788550888 (Cloth)
9781788550895 (Kindle)
9781788550901 (Epub)
9781788550918 (PDF)

British Library Cataloguing in Publication Data
An entry can be found on request

Library of Congress Cataloging in Publication Data
An entry can be found on request

Typeset in Sabon LT Std 11/15 pt

Jacket front: Portrait of Benedict Kiely (1977), Edward McGuire RHA (1932–1986). Reproduced with the kind permission of Tresa Browne. Courtesy of the National Library of Ireland.

Jacket back: Courtesy of the Estate of Stephen McKenna and Kerlin Gallery, Dublin.

CONTENTS

GEORGE O'BRIEN

•

Introduction: Benedict Kiely, Singular and Plural

Age cannot wither him, nor custom stale his infinite variety. A hundred years on, Benedict Kiely remains as good as new – as original, as incorrigible, as inimitable, as necessary. As far as variety is concerned – novelist, short-story writer, critic, memoirist, journalist, broadcaster, travel writer – few, if any, Irish writers of any time can match his diligence and productivity; he truly was the 'all-rounder' Brian Fallon warmly recalls. The picture of him opening the front door in his pyjamas, given by Colum McCann, may raise a smile, but Ben had been writing all night: that adds admiration to the smile. Nor should the range of his work be regarded as mere facility, enviable for its focus, application and professionalism though his versatility is. As well as the typical ease and fluency of Ben's writing, there is also a catholicity about all that he produced which calls to mind more significant elements of the man and his work. Such scope suggests a rejection of narrowness, a hospitality to different forms and materials, an aversion to generic limitation, and an imaginative inclination to cross borders rather than be confined by them.

1

Not surprisingly, then, copiousness of mind and openness of heart are the Kiely attributes that recur time and again throughout the essays in celebration and commemoration which make up *In a Harbour Green*. By common consent, it seems, these are the terms in which the writer is to be most suitably honoured. Moreover, it also seems that to esteem the writer is to honour the man, for in virtually every case, the essayist recalls the living Ben. The generous Ben – friend to Thomas Kilroy, Christopher Cahill, Brian Fallon and Thomas O'Grady; friend and mentor to Colum McCann and John Wilson Foster; local to look up to for Martina Devlin; cultural phenomenon in the eyes (and ears) of Patricia Craig; literary path-finder for Derek Hand. Once encountered never forgotten, a storyteller who lives on not only in the stories he told but in those that continue to be told about him, a novelist who set out critical criteria by which his own endeavours might be evaluated, a traveller of whom it has been rightly said 'there is no Irish writer whose work is more inextricably woven into the landscape that bred him'[1] and who nevertheless made repeated voyages of discovery in his own country and sang the praises of all its variegated sights, scenes and citizenry. And these variegations, in turn, find further expression in his fertile imagination – most notably in his stories – by being called up in whatever 'ballad, story, rann and song' seems apt, borrowings from a common tongue and a common heritage, their colours and contours enhancing the already rich proceedings. Derek Hand has pointed out 'how difficult it is to separate Benedict Kiely the man from Benedict Kiely the writer'.[2] And, indeed, singularity was Ben's signature, a uniqueness embodying multiplicity, not just in his combination of artistry and personality but in the vivid, continuous, daring interplay that he maintained between them. That vital presence, and the concerns which energised it, are what the present work, in appreciation and remembrance, salutes.

If Benedict Kiely was a man who had faith in the word – and not many would argue otherwise, seeing as he wore his belief on his sleeve, nowhere more so, perhaps, than in the mixture of courage and rage that fuels *Proxopera* and *Nothing Happens in Carmincross* – then, for the world at large, the word was synonymous with the voice – 'that amber voice' in Thomas Kilroy's warm and winning phrase.[3] Ben's voice was a kind of a place, or at least a space, where man and writer became indistinguishable, where memory (his repertoire) and the moment (his listeners) became one – to borrow from John Wilson Foster's essay on the meditations upon time that are so central to Ben's imagination. And like who knows how many thousands of others, I, too, had the good fortune to hear what it could do.

One particularly memorable occasion was at the launch of Austin Clarke's *Selected Poems* in the Palace Bar – Dublin, where else? – in June 1991. There was a handsome turn-out, I remember, and James Plunkett did the launching honours – one of Dublin's own speaking for another. There was the usual white wine, sweet and warm. Books were on sale, and maybe sold. Groups formed and reformed around the room as the crowd, having done its duty by poetry, smiled and chatted, all civil and sociable, and before too very long began to drift away. It was as the gathering was thinning that I noticed Ben, who evidently had not mingled; indeed, he seemed not even to have stirred from his place. He was gazing steadily into the middle distance, and on either side of him there were a few others, their heads attentively inclined towards him, for what he was doing was paying a tribute of his own to the poet who was being fêted.

Many years before, he had made it known that 'Mr Clarke is today the greatest living Irish poet and one of the few writers living in Ireland who could be described as a beneficent encouraging influence'.[4] Now he was doing the one thing the event lacked – reciting a poem. For the life of me I can't remember which poem it was. But I remember that the voice was low, slow, steady, intent, somewhat mesmerising in its apparent inability to halt or falter. This was no performance, but homage, and who knew the difference better than the reciter himself. It was as though he was bearing witness to Clarke's own state at the prospect of meeting Pablo Neruda: 'how could I know him / If not by song?' The whole thing hardly took more than a minute, but the act of remembrance, the commemoration of the poet's gift, the uses of culture, the filling or should I say fulfilling of the moment, will always remain. A statement of presence, or – to borrow again, this time from Colum McCann – 'a wakeful grace' was being enacted through communication. And all without glass in hand or roistering note, those two apparently inescapable features of stories about Ben, so much so that it would make you wonder when he ever had time enough or head clear enough to write anything at all, despite his body of work being there for all to see. Although let it be said also, on Ben's behalf, that 'books are wonderful and enriching, but ... life – if properly lived, if lived with style – is the thing.'[5]

Nor was carousing required to attract the thousands who delighted in Ben's expansive, digressive, anecdotal-to-a-fault voice on the radio. He had been on the wireless his whole career long, pretty much, so any thought that when he became a regular on *Sunday Miscellany* he was somehow offering a diminished expression of himself would be not only hopelessly inaccurate and unacceptably presumptuous but would also condescend inexcusably to those listeners across the country relishing his discourses – let the subject be the Formorians, Douglas Hyde, *Ulysses* or 'funny philosophers', or just about everything in between. Besides, there was something more to those talks of his than a diverting use of learning lightly worn and warmly transmitted, though that in itself was plenty. The extra element was just the voice's very presence. A Northern voice. A voice whose Northernness persisted, one might say – persisted, that is, in dealing with matters and in tones that were very much the antithesis of a good deal of what was emanating at the time from Ben's native province. The matters and tones from the North caused him serious chagrin, and his broadcasts – in their relish of plenitude, the unexpected, vagaries and the sheer scope of different items available for rumination and mulling over – intended, perhaps unconsciously, to counteract them.

Here was a contrary identity, unbounded and affirmative, and voice as generous invitation, in quality and character as far from Northern noise (verbal and otherwise) as it was possible to be, a living instrument which in timbre and delivery lent to the objects of its attention a breath of fresh air, a kind of intellectual neighbourliness, and to the individual listener a Sunday outing to things possessed in common. These were gather-round-me moments, and gather audiences did. To think back to the context in which the broadcasts were given and to regard them as offerings of a good word in a Northern accent (and, as such, comparable to what Seamus Heaney was giving in his packed-out readings) is to value them anew. Hallmark of his latter years these talks may have been, and the public at large certainly remembers Ben for them. But they were also yet one more expression of what had long been evident in Ben Kiely's work: that, where he was concerned, neither the voice nor its owner knew no borders. Or, rather, if they did, it was not to be either defied or defeated by them.

THE VIEW FROM THE TERRACE

As all the world knows, Ben was from Omagh, and equally well known is how he held in memory dear the rivers and hills of home, the town's passageways and public buildings, the various populations and their many ways of living, and by no means least the townlands round about whose names ring out like a peal of bells as the tenor of a particular work requires. The cartography of affection for his first landscape that so much of Ben's work fleshes out gathers together matters little and big into one unified act of *pietas*, whereby person and place belong to one another, each contributing to the other's story to their mutual sustainment. This mapping of attachment constitutes a vision, of course, an outlook and perspective won from certain raw materials, exacting a toll in effort and dedication which itself is a measure of purpose and value. Yes, Ben is from Omagh and – to adapt Martina Devlin's witty dual-language play on the words 'from' and 'out of' – Omagh is from him; he has gifted the place back to itself.

It's a gift that sees the place in certain kinds of light, as is the nature of visions. So, part of Ben's work of creation consisted of dealing with the knowledge that some elements of his cultural and historical patrimony permanently overshadowed others. And one of the most obvious palls cast was the fact that the life into which he was born was divided. Ben's was the first generation to know this split as a juridical, political, administrative reality, to grow in awareness that suspicion and bad blood, hatred and hostility were no mere personal reactions but structures of feeling intended to protect and defend one side or another in 'the riven land'.[6] Obviously, it would be entirely too reductive to think of Ben Kiely's artistic accomplishments and cultural standing from the perspective of partition. Yet, at the same time, there persists throughout his writing a consciousness of limits, constrictions, separations, disharmony, houses divided and community fault-lines, out of which emerge those areas of darkness referred to by Thomas Kilroy in his essay. Clearly, such areas may have many origins, and their presence hardly eclipses the summery air of childhood and youth which often are the breath of Ben's work. Still,

No matter how sunny and easy-going Omagh was in his young days, the division was always there, the conqueror's flag flew from the public buildings, the bottle-green constabulary carried their master's guns on the streets; it was an imperfect world, offering only a skew glimpse of idyll.[7]

Whatever kind of mark it left on him, this context provided the basis for Ben's first two books, *Counties of Contention* and *Land Without Stars*, the first subtitled 'A Study of the Origins and Implications of the Partition of Ireland' and the second a story of two young brothers' responses – fight or flight – to those implications. The fact that Ben saw the six counties to be a matter of contention suggests a sense of at least uneasiness and unfinished business concerning his home place, a sense that these two books often express in terms of naming and identity and the arbitrariness and uncertainty they underwrite. And the title *Land Without Stars* implicitly names the Northern landscape in which its characters contend, with the title itself drawn from a poem by Aodhagán Ó Rathaille, an echo from the Gaelic past, continuity with which is tacitly proposed as one position contrary to the occlusions of the novel's 1930s setting.[8] In their acts of naming, or renaming, both works address matters of belonging and being at home, not only indicating barriers to affiliation but also wondering what good is there in such barriers, and what good will come of them. A partial answer that must be considered is given in the ending of *Land Without Stars* with one of the Quinn brothers consigned, after an exchange of fire with the authorities, to permanent darkness.

Cultural, intellectual, ideological and historical concerns inform these first two books of Ben's – books whose originality has perhaps been insufficiently recognised; they are not only his first publications but among the first to discuss Northern Ireland from the viewpoint of a member of the community which was at the receiving end of that entity's policies and practices. In addition to those general considerations, both works depict the intimacy of division. Martina Devlin refers to a relevant passage showing Omagh's split-level geography. This passage is reworked in *Land Without Stars*:

> Devlin Street hadn't changed. The same small huckster's shop standing apart and separate. Facing it a block of grey houses, silent, with half-drawn blinds. All Protestants that lived there; their houses had a solemn, fur-capped Calvinistic appearance. The shoemaker's, the forge, the poultry-dealer's yard, the block of white shabby houses. All Catholics ... Every inch of the street, every doorway had its meaning.[9]

Very much a part of that meaning is what Ben identified as 'the interweaving of love and imagination with locality [which] is something that our ancestors were particularly good at',[10] with that ancestral connection suggesting (as in the use of Ó Rathaille) a means of going beyond the dispensation of the present. And go beyond it Ben did with that very same interweaving. Even so, however, it has also to be allowed that Ben, 'to judge from his writing ... has lived his life ... in the shadow'.[11] And, alas, the shadow would never quite go away, as Thomas Kilroy's essay reminds us through its commentary on the affronts to life, limb, agency and habitat which form the distressing subject matter and embittered outlook of the novels with which Ben more or less concluded his output, *Proxopera* and *Nothing Happens in Carmincross*. In these works, as courageous in their way as the two which launched him as a writer to be reckoned with, it doesn't matter where that shadow originates. What matters is its capacity to blacken and obliterate one way of life in the name of imposing another. The enraged and lamenting Ben who sounds out in the final novels is somebody for whom such darkness is the antithesis of the human capacity for reconciling differences and visions of wholeness.

But perhaps darkness and division were a spur, not necessarily required, but an acknowledgment of the fallible way of the world. 'Those divisions he characterised as projecting themselves into the spirit', Martina Devlin writes. Ben was there to contend with them as best he could, his imagination (always as much moral as aesthetic, which is saying something for a writer as style-conscious and structurally adept as he was) the place where the forces contended. Something of a model of this activity can be seen in *Poor Scholar*, the story of his avatar, William Carleton, and of how his was a life divided between communal affections and the ego's goads. Gerald Dawe's essay traces the tissue of cultural and indeed political connection between Carleton and his fellow countyman, a connection that also speaks to other North–South literary journeys and careers, as well as to borderland tonalities and frequencies registered by the poet's ear.

Dawe's attunement to a regional accent is a reminder, as well, that *Poor Scholar* is a silence-breaking work not only with respect to Carleton and his pre-Famine background but to the living community in the Clogher Valley and surroundings, as well as to the virtually unspeakable means by which that community came to grief. One aim discernible in writing of such matters is to remove whatever roadblocks might have existed in the contemplation of this material and in Carleton's acts of faithful, if over-zealous, witness to them. The book's publication in the centenary year of 'the blackest year of black famine'[12] vindicates that aim, is in its own way a commentary on silence, and in addition testifies to the cultural value of memory as exemplified by both Carleton and his commemorator – Carleton's 'types are valid enough to this day'.[13] And in contemplating the psychological and physical suffering in Carleton's pages, conditions heightened by the author's own confrontation of them, there is more than enough of shadow and darkness.

One reason that Ben regarded Carleton as 'among the greatest, perhaps the greatest, writer of fiction that Ireland has given to the English language'[14] may be that Carleton, in both pre-Famine and post-, is in the nature of a monument to continuity. In that sense he is a figure who resists the historical truism that the Famine brought about a devastating breach in Irish life and culture. Not that the truism doesn't hold good. At the same time, however, in the combination of remembering his own people and the distance from which, in his maturity, he regarded them there is a way of acknowledging division and defying its ostensible finality. This awareness of belonging in tandem with separation is also noteworthy for informing the perspectives of *Modern Irish Fiction: A Critique*. Here, it might be said that the breach is reproduced in the two schools of Irish fiction that the book identifies, one typified in the work of Daniel Corkery, with its fidelity to land, people and tradition, the other represented in the writing of James Joyce and its expressions of departure articulated through ego, exile and modernist prosodies.

In his critique, Ben speaks fluently of both, aware equally of their cultural and aesthetic dimensions, and in a sense occupying a place between them, as though acknowledging divisions between sheep and goats and yet declining to be a member of one species or the other, thus quietly but nevertheless firmly asserting his own artistic independence. Yet, the awareness of a tension, or split, between artistic objectives and cultural pieties is present throughout, again suggesting an orientation around ideas of incompleteness and wholeness, continuity and change, the home ground and the international scene, an awareness ultimately deployed to nourish and sustain a conception of a diverse but unified body of work that might be thought of as a prototype in imaginative prose of a national literature. A site not of seven streams meeting, perhaps, but of several – as they do for Ben, unforgettably, around Omagh.

But in Omagh, too, divisions persist. By virtue of remaining unnamed, the town in Ben's second novel may not be Omagh. But nobody believes this. It's a town where division seems to have become internalised, existing within families, among lovers, between classes. The social and cultural rifts of *Land Without Stars* are also present, but they are not to the fore. Instead, the manner in which characters choose to make their lives (or try to choose) constitutes an emotional tug of war, with those who stay at home diminished, while the one who leaves finds only the exterior darkness of the Second World War. There is a living future in the son who will never know his father, but that same father is a missing element in both private and communal life. And what is missing creates and perpetuates the flawed marriage for which the partners in it opted. To tease out a parable from *In a Harbour Green* would be a tedious and reductive task, no doubt, but it is also difficult to overlook the presence and the power of inadequately consummated choices, or to take the title entirely at its poetically evocative word.

THE SHORTEST WAY HOME

Like Carleton, Kavanagh and Kiely before him, Peter Quinn, the protagonist of *Land Without Stars*, leaves his Northern hearth and home for Dublin and a writing career. On arrival, all he can see is green, 'a soft green that soaked into brain and body', which not only lends the young man's outlook an affirmative and appeasing coloration but also reminds him that home had never been like this. Peter's arrival in the capital marks the end of his story. In all likelihood, however, the city proved to be no harbour green for him – at least judging by the portrait of Dublin painted in most of Ben's 1950s novels, the characters of which generally seem out of place, hampered physically and psychologically, and lacking in direction as they face the challenges of living lives of their own in an indifferent environment.

And for all the many years he lived there, Ben, too, never entirely belonged in Dublin. Fond of the city as he was, and much as he appreciated what it stood for, historically, culturally and politically, he could never be as attached to the place as he was to his origins.[15] He might acknowledge being a Dubliner, but he knew that this was not the same thing at all as the genuine article, a Dublinman.[16] Naturally, he was very much alive to Dublin's social and topographical amenities, from its night life to restorative days out amidst mountain greenery and the grasslands of Meath. But the vivid descriptions of these venues in, for instance, *Call for a Miracle* and *Honey Seems Bitter* are counterpointed by the complications in the characters' lives which also arise even as they are out enjoying themselves. Continuing with the perspective of *In a Harbour Green*, the stories of these lives are essentially inward, almost entirely untouched by the contexts and communities in which, willy-nilly, they go about their business. Indeed, Dublin often seems a nameless place, as much site as city, a realm in which the realities of world, flesh and devil make themselves known to often young and morally ill-equipped characters. (This realm might be interestingly compared to the metropolitan badlands of Graham Greene's novels, with which Ben's work also shares a concern with the workings of conscience.)

The characters' difficulties, which include difficulties of attachment, fidelity, security and self-belief, are more exacerbated than in Ben's first two novels. Divided against themselves, remote from families and estranged from spouses, separated from each other by social class, these urbanites may well be seen to embody the existential anxieties typically thought of as characteristic of modern life. In his essay, Derek Hand speaks of 'the struggle towards modernity', and that's the story that Ben's Dublin novels tell, right enough: the story of struggle. To find out what they're made of, and to survive that discovery, often forms the core of the characters' stories while they drift on the waters of a harbour that exposes rather than shelters them, and as they contend with a moral landscape which evidently cannot, or will not, foster such enabling energies as choice, decision-making and commitment, by which they might become more complete.

Speaking of energy, the fact that Ben had the reserves to write at all while holding down a full-time job as a newspaperman is worthy of note, particularly given the differences in idiom and address between those two pursuits. And here it might be noted that writing novels could itself lead to a sense of division between writer and reader, and also between him and his contexts – his literary home ground, as it were – owing to the operation of the Censorship Board.[17] Yet, if his day job was conducive to making a Dubliner of Ben, the city of *Call for a Miracle* and *Honey Seems Bitter* is abandoned with an almost formal finality in the novel that follows them, *The Cards of the Gambler*. This work's eschatological themes and innovative construction is a striking departure from its predecessors and is commonly regarded as one of Ben's finest accomplishments in the form, although it also remains related to the earlier novels through its various structural and narrative uses of displacement and relocation.

A principle of diversity and interrelatedness informs the novel in the ways it aligns an ancient, local Irish folktale with the European Faust legend and how it combines a contemporary Irish context with continental ones. At a thematic level, in *The Cards of the Gambler* universal tropes of loss and recuperation recur, and this recurrence is reproduced at the artistic level with a substitution of plot as conventionally understood with a method of layering, with the result that 'Kiely has joined the arts of the storyteller and the novelist ... very different, and in some ways antagonistic arts, issuing from different psychic and cultural roots.'[18] This method previews most of Ben's subsequent novels, culminating in the carnival of individual histories – good, bad and indifferent – contained in the 'fictional summing up'[19] of *Dogs Enjoy the Morning*. And the method is also the artistic mainstay of Ben's short stories, where it facilitates the stories' range of temporalities, their intertextual amusements, their episodic structure and their unusually large cast of characters.

Any reading of *There was an Ancient House* or *The Captain with the Whiskers* will show, however, that the uses of intercalation in them is a resource within the material, not a design borrowed from *The Cards of the Gambler* and systematically applied. And like *The Cards of the Gambler* and its predecessors, those two novels are still concerned with issues of world and flesh, while in *The Captain with the Whiskers* we find, in effect, the devil himself, the meaning of which Thomas Kilroy's essay points out. In that novel, and in *There was an Ancient House* as well, a concern with division remains pressing – between the weak flesh and the willing spirit in the latter, between nature and nurture in *The Captain with the Whiskers*. The introduction of a strongly autobiographical note in *There was an Ancient House* and the fact that the evil one in *The Captain with the Whiskers* is already dead at the start of his story both signal that impersonal, conflict-inducing regimes are not necessarily permanent, and that the singular character of the order those powers are able to impose (whether in a good house or a bad one; the novels alternate from one to the other) does not utterly overshadow the diversity that exists beyond their precincts, physical and psychological. It is such signalling that Ben's short stories go on to explore and develop.

As may be seen from how they form a thread through so many of the contributors' thoughts on Ben, the short stories are central to an appreciation of his achievement. And, indeed, who can resist their yarning air, their anecdotes and digressions, their colourful characters, their whole repertoire of verbal forms and resources, the closeness they exhibit to reader and subject alike. Diverting in event, humane in tone, pleasurable in general effect, their appeal speaks for itself. But to think of them solely with regard to their surface properties, or to claim that for an adequate critical assessment of them '[i]t might be more apposite to invoke the Somerville and Ross of *The Irish R.M.* crossed with the *Sportsman's Sketches* of Turgenev',[20] overlooks some of their more telling aspects.

One of those aspects is their reliance on returning. It has been noted that 'a recurrent pattern in [Benedict Kiely's] stories is that of the quest.'[21] The return, however, completes the quest. The stories tell of not only sallying forth for its own sake, but for the sake of coming to terms with what constituted the quest's context and pretext. The quest is local, and the return places that in a different, more comprehensive, perspective. Returning takes various forms – there is the exile's return, the return in memory, the return of a memory, and the failure to return (typically brought up in connection with emigration, and considered a waste). To return has numerous cognates – to regain, renew, re-enter, repossess, reunite and reward, for instance – and these give some suggestion of the activity's significance in the context of Ben's body of work as a whole. For to return, particularly when it is to the primal ground of home (as is so often the case), is to see the place in two ways, in the here and now as well as in the there and then. Perhaps for that reason, many of Ben's stories realign material first glimpsed in his early novels, dwelling now less on protagonists and family dynamics than on highlighting what might be thought of as minor characters and community relations. On the face of it, this dual focus suggests another manifestation of division, and up to a point the stories concede as much in their various acknowledgments of remembrance and loss, as John Wilson Foster's essay details. Yet, at the same time, the return is also a path to renegotiation, to making peace (as best one can) with a variety of legacies, and with respect to the art of storytelling, to allow the guiding voice and its resources to flower above the seedbed of realities from which it grows.

Tolerance, acceptance and reconciliation are the stories' general tendencies, despite the difficulty with which they are won, and despite the fragile coalition of elements that sustain them – the myriad details noted in passing (and thus preserved), the gallery of minor characters (commemorated in their ostensible insignificance), the constant borrowings from songbooks and every other kind of book (dissolving on being uttered but enduring through print). People and things that do not necessarily or obviously belong together inhabit the same discursive space (which, for the most part, we can call Omagh), maintaining their distinctiveness, while at the same time, as though they know no better, contributing unwittingly yet also as of right to the broad narrative current. Caring for the youngster, the narrator of 'The Shortest Way Home' recalls himself as having been led by his tutelary spirit, Big May, into the world, into loss and leaving. Yet, in return (or on remembering), he again sees himself and his pals '[a]ll together ... in the green light'. Ben, the storyteller, makes himself available as a meeting place for his dual perspective. He is the place where differences are allowed, indeed encouraged, to live side by side. Perhaps this moral of the stories – one of many, without a doubt – has something to do with Ben's point that '[s]ometime in the 1960s it seemed to me that people in the northeast corner were beginning to talk to each other as they had always done in Omagh, my hometown, a pretty civilised place.'[22] And perhaps it was to acknowledge that accommodating, non-discriminatory largesse that a friend appreciatively wrote, 'Ben stands firmly at the extreme centre, to which he has been led, perhaps driven, by long experience and a close and empathetic observation of people and places.'[23] And while in one sense it may be thought of as the space occupied by the storyteller, the *seanchaí*, mediating between his listeners and tradition, the centre also offers the idea of a place where various points meet, even though regarded separately they have never seemed particularly inclined to do so.

'AND AS I RODE BY'

So many stories, so many journeys, so many stories with journeys in them, so many journeys turning into stories ... To return, of course, is also to travel, and the reconstitutive potential of returning is also present in Ben's travel writings, the form in which he was first published (as Brian Fallon's reference to the essay 'Land Without Stars' reminds us)[24] and a form of writing in which he continued to publish throughout his career. Ben's very voice is replete with travel elements, issuing invitations to visit, providing the visitor with *vade mecum*s, branching off the main narrative path to sing, allude or quote, or simply to take in the sheer abundance of suggestive instances to be found along whatever green road he happened to be on.

Few were the roads he did not find green. The embrace of place that the stories delight in also applies to the towns and townlands to which his road-trips bring him resulting, as far as his travels in Ireland go, in feats of association and connection. As he wrote, 'everything in Ireland reminds me of something else'.[25] Travel makes links possible, opens routes of thought and reflection – or, to call up the cliché, broadens the mind, which if Ben did not necessarily set out to accomplish, he ended up exemplifying in the ease with which he fell in with strangers, guided guests and consistently remained receptive, invariably willing to discover and to be surprised, always alive to whatever the world of the moment bestowed.

Roving out and roaming out seems to have been virtually a historical destiny for Ben, and in its way *And as I Rode by Granard Moat* bears out this notion. A tour of the country in rhyme and song, the book is in the nature of a map of common ground made up of musical and narrative notations, with the bond between words and music so basic and so interwoven that it would take obtuseness in a rare degree to resist what they make up together. Almost all the material featured is a hymn to the local, or a hymn to remembrance of the local, but while local flavour and colour shine through undimmed, the whole that they comprise is more than the sum of the parts. It's a journey through a country that is both recognisable and unfamiliar, a cartography of endearment and uplift, a banner waving in the face of the bloodshed and unhappiness with which a certain amount of its contents deal. As such, the book may seem to be an extrapolation of the distinguishing yet integrating method of Ben's stories: 'I may seem deliberately capricious in the order and arrangement of the poems, songs and recitations; but there is, I hope, a certain method in that'.[26] And as in the stories, with their palimpsest-like accretions of difference and commonality, the seemingly happenstance nature of how memory, language and place are brought together to be voiced has something of the possibility of appeasement to it, and in that, a certain wonder, all the more noteworthy for being unassuming, popular, commonplace and local. Or, to put it another way, perhaps: 'Drumquin, you're not a city / But you're all the world to me'.[27] Ben wandered well beyond Drumquin, of course, and out of Ireland as well, to America, that traveller's paradise, whose seemingly inexhaustible heterogeneity is not only confined within a single national territory but appears to define the place, an *ur*-landscape of travel containing everything the traveller could desire and announcing that fact as brazenly as possible. As Paul Clements points out in his essay, the carnivalesque side of Ben's imagination was greatly stimulated by the panorama presented. How many miles he covered it is impossible to say, but from his 'Letters from America' (references to which by both Paul Clements and Christopher Cahill whets the appetite for their republication) it does appear that in his various Stateside sojourns Ben touched on all the cardinal points and a great deal in between. Of course, the many-sidedness of the place appealed to him, and it comes as no surprise that he took to the road on public transport, which not only made panoramic views of the enormous continent available but, just as important, if not more so, provided him with people to talk to (his Irish sorties had already demonstrated that travel without company was, for Ben, more or less a contradiction in terms). The image of him as a Huckleberry Finn in his forties 'lighting out for the new territory', as Mark Twain's hero did, is difficult to resist.

Both the opening up of the vast land before him and his own opening out to greet it undoubtedly had an effect on his sense of new possibilities. After all, he was just past the age when life was supposed to begin. And there were other types of venturing to go with the geographical kind – in classrooms, in academia more generally, in a different literary culture, particularly through the academics and intellectuals associated with the *Hollins Critic*, a well-known journal based at Hollins College in southern Virginia, Ben's first American employer. There is also another dimension to Ben's time in America, a historical one, marked by the rise of youth culture, the Vietnam War and protests against it, and the civil rights movement. America, too, was a divided country; indeed, taken together, Paul Clements's and Christopher Cahill's essays give some inklings of the two countries that Ben encountered – on the one hand, the expansive, welcoming and larger-than-life one; on the other, a place that was excessive, stupid and dangerous. Both, we learn, are represented in Ben's 'Letters from America'; and in other writings, too, it is clear that he was aware that, for all the freedom that America could boast of, for some it was a land of the free in name only.[28]

Yet Ben also had much to offer, not only as a guest and a personality but as a writer, too – an Irish writer, at that. His numerous contributions to the *New York Times Book Review* and other periodicals were not just indications of his novelty value as a spokesman on Irish literature and history. His articles and reviews also helped him see his standing and what it represented in a fresh light. Distance allowed for a certain reorientation, and this too perhaps encouraged him on the path he had taken to suspend, or rethink, his novel-writing and instead develop the aesthetic informing his stories.[29]

To examine in necessary detail the cultural and artistic interchanges between Ben and his various American milieux would obviously be a complex undertaking. But in its various leavings and returns, its replacing of one expressive form with another, with accompanying changes in his narrator's materials and tone, together with a greater emphasis on such fundamentals of travel as the temporary and the transitory, it doesn't seem too much to suggest that America was a turn in the road for Ben. And it may be, too, that Ben at home and in the company of American friends, in the picture painted in Christopher Cahill's essay, sustained the sharpened curiosity and sense of discovery – or, perhaps, uncovering – of his American experiences, and helped to bring to the fore, among other things, a pleasure principle which, hitherto, had not been as marked a feature of his work, assiduously though his characters in his novels might have sought it. The traveller returned, thankfully, but it was a very good thing, too, that he brought back with him an expansiveness, a venturesomeness, and not only an idea of 'what America has gatherumed and mixumed in a short two centuries'[30] but how the idea might be applied to advantage with respect to his own country, allowing the many and allowing also for its potential to become one. In all that, too, Ben showed his suppleness of mind, his artistic resourcefulness, and his multiplicity. And nowhere did those qualities shine through more than in the realisation that the blend and braid of life could be most rewardingly accommodated and most winningly exemplified by realities he respected to such a degree that he transfigured them, the realities of the town he loved so well that it glowed in his consciousness – and continues to do so in ours – as a harbour green.

It seems no more than fitting that a book commemorating Benedict Kiely's centenary should be many-sided. Friend and colleague, Northerner and Southerner, writer of fiction and of non-fiction equally evocative and thoughtful, exhilarating travelling companion and contemplator of home-town intimacies, a man of conscience and a man of wit – these Bens are honoured here. As are others, too. And no matter how many more there were, there would probably still be a feeling that the measure of him, man and writer, had not been reached. Further efforts await, no doubt, as his second century dawns. And it's to be hoped that the contributions to *In a Harbour Green* point out pathways to greater appreciation and increased regard. Ben, at one hundred, remains as vivid and as vital in our culture and outlook as he did when gracing us with his presence. And on he fares, his voice, his words, resounding.

•

Benedict Kiely in His Own Time

Benedict Kiely – always 'Ben' to friends and acquaintances, and to many people besides – was one of the last of the great all-rounders of Irish literature. I use the phrase deliberately. It is a virtual commonplace nowadays that ours is a specialist age and, in fact, it is difficult to escape the conviction that the literary scene – for lack of a better phrase – has both narrowed and hardened steadily, and seems likely to go on doing so. I make no claim to originality in saying so, since the facts speak increasingly for themselves. There seems to be less and less space for the intelligent middlebrow writer or for the literary all-rounder in the old, familiar but still respectful sense. Even biography, once a virtual monopoly of the professional man of letters, has become a specialised field in which research is almost everything, with readability at a discount.

No doubt there is both gain and loss in this, but the fact remains that the loss is considerable. A Belloc or a Chesterton, for instance, could scarcely exist today – or if they did, they certainly would not command the attention or respect they once did. Nor could a Mencken or a Van

Wyck Brooks. Even such a superb all-round professional as Somerset Maugham continues to be read almost solely for his novels, while the bulk of his other writings is scarcely to be found even in book-barrows – insofar as such things still exist. Yet in my own youth I read with absorption the weekly review-articles by V.S. Pritchett in the *New Statesman*, just as I read Ernest Newman's music column in the *Sunday Times*, or the art criticism of Patrick Heron. In retrospect, many of us received our cultural initiation through such non-academic channels.

This rather lengthy prelude is not meant to suggest that Benedict Kiely is to be discussed in a middlebrow context, which is largely a thing of the past, or at best of the recent past. Most emphatically, this is not the intention. At the moment, his ultimate status as a fiction-writer has not yet been quite 'finalised' (horrible word, but hard to avoid), though lately there has been a flow of reprints, and his short stories have been collected in a bulky paperback. There can be little doubt, however, that the finest of the novels belong on a shelf of their own, and that they have already outlived most Irish fiction of the last fifty or sixty years. Collections of his essays and occasional writings are also appearing, with material for further compilations readily available. But other facets of his work – Kiely the literary critic – one of the best non-academic ones of his time, though he had his blind spots, like everybody else; Kiely the effective rediscoverer of William Carleton; Kiely the author of a deeply thoughtful survey of Irish fiction – do not as yet feature prominently enough in literary and cultural debate, though, of course, this situation will and must change.[1]

Benedict Kiely, in short, is one of the great, multi-gifted bookmen and his style and personality are inherent in almost everything he wrote, whether you choose to call a sizeable portion of it journalism or occasional writings. His huge output cannot be divided up, since the whole of it remains more or less indivisible, regardless of the immediate context in which specific pieces were produced. In this, he resembles William Hazlitt – partly Irish, by the way – who all his life remained passionate about literature and also could make practically any subject absorbing to the plain reader, from prize-fighting in a muddy, trampled field to a House of Commons debate. Ben's writings are very much like the man himself, even in their occasional oddities and obliquities, and they are also the products of a cultural personality steeped in the literature of the English language, whether in its Anglo-Saxon, Anglo-Irish and Gaelicised, or modern American forms.

Indeed, he spent long periods in America and knew its literature as few people outside universities do. I can bear witness to this, since Ben was constantly in the company of American writers and academics, particularly in Dublin. I even sat in on a good many of their sessions together, usually over lunches at which the wine and talk flowed between volubly erudite interruptions. Yet, scholarly conviviality apart, there is plenty of evidence to show Kiely's affinity with things American, and his literary standing there has always been much higher than in Britain (although he is not alone in this; Thomas Kinsella is another case in point). Ben was also a friend or acquaintance of many American writers, including even the reclusive Flannery O'Connor, and was proud of having met in old age that unique survivor of

Paris and the Golden Twenties, Glenway Wescott, whose book of haunting short stories, *Good-bye, Wisconsin*, as well as his brilliant volume of literary criticism, *Images of Truth*, seem to me among the most neglected of American classics.[2]

Kiely earned much, or even most, of his living as a journalist with three of Dublin's leading newspapers, the *Catholic Standard*, the *Irish Independent*, and *The Irish Press*, of which he became the Literary Editor. This meant that a certain proportion of his output was, inevitably, produced for the moment. But this does not mean, or even imply, that it was written from that dubious and generally uncritical area, the top of his head. He was too much the professional to ignore his duty to the reading public, whoever or whatever the immediate public consisted of. Kiely never manifested any pose whatever of cultural or other superiority, but instead felt himself at one – and at ease – with the Man in the Street. Born in Omagh, County Tyrone – one of the two counties of Northern Ireland to have a Catholic majority, the other being Fermanagh – he grew up in a society in which he and his kind were very much underdogs; and his lifelong sympathies were broad and democratic, even tilting towards populism. Though republican violence nauseated him, he was bitterly critical of the bigoted, undemocratic Stormont regime and considered its collapse inevitable and not too far distant.

Kiely was destined to write and could not have done otherwise, even if he briefly studied to be a Jesuit. Ill health and other factors put an end to that, though I did sense something curiously clerical in his personality. I do not refer here to that outworn cliché, the Spoiled Priest, or to any suggestion of inner guilt or hidden inhibition. There was none of that; the man plainly enjoyed life and lived it to the full, and even beyond it. The clerical element was elusive and indefinable, but it was there nonetheless and was even, in some way or other, part of his moral being.

If he did not actually lisp in numbers, like Pope, at least he must have thought from early on in phrases, sentences or even whole paragraphs. His chief problem was never verbal inhibition or short-windedness; it was rather the polar opposite, the need to temper his natural loquacity and urge to communicate. At the same time, any Hemingway-style cult of terseness or clipped understatement definitely would not have been his style. In his fiction, Kiely did not think in linear terms or rational progressions, let alone the easily-seen-through plotting of the average novel. This was not a failure on his part, more an awareness of life's inconsequentiality or even the sheer irrationality of human nature itself. He could tell a story straight when it suited his artistic aim, but more often he worked indirectly and with an apparent casualness which, nonetheless, left few loose ends behind, though it could leave things unspoken yet implicit.

I once discussed with the late Anthony Cronin Ben's ultimate standing as a writer vis-à-vis those two constantly linked figures, Frank O'Connor and Seán O'Faoláin. Both men were regarded not only as the twin giants of the Irish short story but as virtual keepers of the Irish intellectual conscience, insofar as such a thing existed. Personally, I have always had some doubts as to what extent this very high estimate was justified, though most of the reading and thinking Irish public never appeared either to qualify or question it. This attitude on their part seems slightly odd, in retrospect. Cronin – a clear-headed, though sometimes unduly negative, critic – emphatically came down on Kiely's side against the Big Guns. He praised him as being a far more natural writer than O'Faoláin, whose prose style he considered laboured and self-conscious. As for O'Connor, Cronin admired relatively few of the short stories, seeing in them too many of the tricks and mannerisms of an actor or seasoned professional broadcaster who knew his public. (Ben himself, it should be said, was a notable radio performer, nature having gifted him with a resonant voice as well as a sense of timing. That deep, purring Tyrone accent!) Cronin admitted, and even praised, O'Faoláin's important role as a polemical writer, someone who spoke out on matters from which all too many Irish people averted their heads and hurriedly passed by. This, however, belonged in a context which Cronin had witnessed at first hand in the old days of the *Bell* magazine, days which were well in the past when he and I spoke.

Of his own generation of novelists, Kiely probably stood closest to Kate O'Brien, all the more so since they both suffered from that Cromwell's Curse of philistinism, the Irish Censorship Board.[3] They were also close friends and colleagues to the end, in spite of character differences. For a time, O'Brien even stole some of Ben's thunder, since she too was a public (or at least a semi-public) personality and, in an essential sense, represented the intelligent, convent-educated woman who also had a mind very much her own and allowed few obstacles to hinder her from expressing it. Kate O'Brien is still a key voice of her time – even a key witness, one might say – but somehow without defining that time, or anchoring it in some final, clinching sense. She remains a signpost, so to speak, rather than a stopping place.

Francis MacManus, the Kilkenny writer who became a power in Radio Éireann for several decades, always had a circle of admirers, and Ben was firmly among their number, as was the Athlone novelist and Ben's close friend John Broderick. MacManus's appeal today, I believe, is to a shrinking or minority taste, since provincial Ireland has changed so hugely since he wrote, and the old religious anxieties and tensions no longer speak to us as they once did. At the other end of the scale from both MacManus and Kate O'Brien is Elizabeth Bowen, as representative of upper-class Protestant Ireland as MacManus is of its antithesis, small-town Catholic Ireland. A leading Irish novelist, John Banville, recently told me how much he respected and admired Bowen's *The Last September*. So her name, obviously, is still in the ring. Bowen's career lay largely within the context of the English writing of her time – that is to say, among the cliques, salons and power politics of London, an ultra-competitive milieu where she still managed to hold her own, or rather more than that. For this and other reasons, any comparison between her fiction and Kiely's novels is almost impossible, each author speaking for wholly different worlds, both socially and emotionally. One comparison I would make is between Bowen's and Kiely's short stories. As a whole, hers compare poorly with his in invention and originality. I say this because during my years at the *Irish Times* I was once given a volume of Bowen's stories to review. Quite bluntly, I was shocked to find how flatly derivative many of them were, ranging from Bloomsbury-style preciosity to near-pastiches of O'Faoláin and the Cork School generally.

Compared with its plenitude of good, or even major, poets, Ireland does not offer a great range of novelists. The name of Joyce, of course, will crop up at once. But he remains an outsider – a giant outsider, admittedly, like the great auk – whose life and mentality were largely continental rather than Irish. He had the occasional home follower, such as Brian O'Nolan and Samuel Beckett, but otherwise he seems like a creature from another planet. And the nineteenth century – Griffin, Carleton, the Banim brothers, Kickham, Lover and Lever – seems inescapably provincial and second-rate, notwithstanding Ben's high estimation of Carleton and his refusal to dismiss Lever.[4] Maria Edgeworth's novels rival Trollope's as social history, but her limitations as a storyteller and psychologist tether her tightly to her age, even if her *Castle Rackrent* remains a fixture with period specialists. By contrast, Somerville and Ross, who started in the Victorian Age and reached into the post-colonial one, gave us not only the marvellous *Irish R.M.* stories but also a few genuinely great novels, most notably *The Real Charlotte*. And while George Moore's *Hail and Farewell* trilogy towers above his other writings, as a fiction-writer per se he still ranks high, with several of his lesser-known novels awaiting intelligent rediscovery, as Kiely was well aware.

He read all these authors, of course, and many more, including those of his native province such as Shan F. Bullock and Forrest Reid. English fiction Ben knew from top to bottom and he was also conversant with European fiction, which he read – presumably – in translation.[5] His English contemporaries were unavoidable, and Graham Greene, isolated in his stance as a Catholic writer in a generally hostile milieu, became a key figure to Irish writers, critics and journalists from the 1940s onwards. And in the immediate post-war years, the novels of François Mauriac, Georges Bernanos and other French Catholic writers were almost *de rigueur* as subject for topical debate in Dublin. (Conor Cruise O'Brien's *Maria Cross: Imaginative Patterns in a Group of Catholic Writers* fanned this interest strongly.) Evelyn Waugh, too, was widely read in Ireland, though it was only in his later years that he was viewed as something higher – and deeper – than merely a smart, brittle, society satirist.

Kiely's own novels at one stage became prey for the Irish censors, but it is easily forgotten that this had its positive side, since repute as an immoral writer could further a man's – or woman's – standing in a good many fields. In fact, banned books had their own followers, who somehow usually tracked them down and acquired them for their shelves (not necessarily for open viewing, however). As for setting up some kind of Order of Excellence in Ben's fiction – a tall order, and I rather quail from it. Should *The Cards of the Gambler* or *The Captain with the Whiskers* head the list? Both books have large followings. But *Honey Seems Bitter* and *There was an Ancient House* well deserve rereading, or simple discovery. A later novel, *Dogs Enjoy the Morning*, is not in my estimation one of the major works but it does have plenty of what rather vulgarly used to be called 'jizz'. I find the very late novels such as *Proxopera* and *Nothing Happens in Carmincross* on the thin side; by the time they appeared, moreover, Kiely had said most of what he had to say or needed to say, and was becoming repetitious. But he was, above all else, a pro; and true-born pros do not hang up their weapons even with old age approaching but go on jousting to the last.

What of Ben's short stories, which a good many people prefer to the novels, although personally I refuse to separate the two? *Ex duobus unum*, in fact. The various individual collections published over the years have now been gathered together in *The Collected Stories of Benedict Kiely*, a monolithic tome which is likely to crowd unstoppably onto Irish bookshelves for decades ahead. But they are simply too many, too contrasting and too dense – or, rather, too rich – to risk any facile generalisations. However, 'A Ball of Malt and Madame Butterfly' surely deserves to be singled out not only for its vitality, but for being so intensely representative. It is, indeed, one of his ultra-typical works.

As already mentioned, Kiely was a valued critic and book reviewer over decades. But it is quite often criticism of a special, personalised type and rather rarely a set-piece. Here I eagerly recommend *A Raid into Dark Corners and Other Essays*, a generous sampling of his thoughts on Irish novelists he cherished, with as well a branching out into memoir as he recalls Brendan Behan, who adored him. For me, the jewel of this collection is an early, lengthy piece about that great and unique seventeenth-century Gaelic poet, Aodhagán Ó Rathaille, aptly entitled 'Land Without Stars', which Kiely wrote chiefly at the instigation of that remarkable man, Father Senan, one-time editor of the *Capuchin Annual* and a born discoverer of talent. The piece typifies Ben's ability to talk with ordinary, unlettered country people and extract facts and folklore from them, and displays as well his powerful sense of history, his almost extra-sensory response to landscape and locality, and his cultural insight. I might even feel tempted – if I were given the choice – to trade one or two of the short stories for this superb recreation of a terrible time for Ireland and of a very great poet. Fortunately, the fullness of Benedict Kiely's body of work means that there is no need to trade.

MARTINA DEVLIN

•

Out of Omagh

When I was a little girl growing up in Omagh, Ben Kiely's name was often heard. It belonged to a man, I was given to understand, whose achievements reflected well on his hometown. At first, I didn't know what he had done; soccer stars, singers and scientists all muddled up together for me. It took a while to join the dots, grasping that the voice on the radio spinning yarns – the one that had my father shushing us as soon as its mournful basso swelled through the room – belonged to this same Ben Kiely. Or Benedict, as the announcer introduced him. Not that anybody in Omagh ever used the full version of his name. Why would they when so many in the town and its hinterland knew his seed and breed, and shared a classroom, played Gaelic football or soccer, cycled the length and breadth of Tyrone, and knew him when he was a youngster with a shock of hair and a civil manner?

Once, he was pointed out to me on the High Street by my father – a man not easily impressed – and I was left in no doubt that here stood a Master. He was a writer below in Dublin, it was explained to me, but – crucially – he was out of Omagh. Wherever he went, he was one of our own.

Our errand took us past the man of letters. As he walked by, my father inclined his head and said, 'Ben'; a slow nod and a likewise sparing 'Francie' was batted back at him. The encounter was as courteous and stately as a gavotte – two middle-aged men from the same small town saluting one another. Following behind, I was tipped into silence by this glimpse of a wider world, filing away a mental picture of someone with eyes that darted here and there, even as he lounged at his ease.

Back home, I scanned the bookshelves and there he was, sandwiched between Maurice Walsh and Frank O'Connor. In multiple. Well-leafed. Each book with that deceptively melancholy face on the dust jacket. In my imagination I had interacted with greatness. That I had done no more than straddle along before him (a verb which the wordsmith in him would like, I suspect), possibly drawing a glance from those light eyes, did nothing to dampen my sense of reverence. Later, I would discover he knew O'Connor and had mentioned the short-story writer in his memoirs. O'Connor, he recalled, was acquainted with W.B. Yeats and fond of remarking: 'As Yeats said to me …' Once, he was asked, with more than a hint of mockery, 'And what did you say to Yeats?' To which he replied, joining in the joke, 'Yes, Mr Yeats.'

Kiely's books shared shelf space with greyhound race cards, the Bible and my mother's collection of photograph albums. Sometimes, I'd take down one of his novels or short-story collections and examine the title and his name on the spine, too young to read their contents but curious about them. By handling his books, I first grasped the notion that writers weren't necessarily dead men and women in frock coats and crinolines – they might be living people whose job was to invent stories, the way my father drove a bus or my uncles worked on London's tall buildings or my grandfather dug gardens. That's when the seeds of my own authorial hopes were watered.

By and by, I found a notebook in my Christmas stocking, on its cover a bird with a swashbuckling air, and decided it was perfect for recording the adventures of a burglar magpie. I consulted one of Kiely's books and proceeded to write Chapter One, Chapter Two and so on, adding The End with a flourish on the final page. This, before a word of the story was composed. Still, I had a framework, inspired by Kiely. In his own phrase, he belonged to 'a world where books mattered' and he made that world important to others. He was one of the people who helped to make it matter to me.

Later, he would prove still more useful as a model because of his versatility – he could turn his hand to radio essays, newspaper articles, novels, short stories and non-fiction, signalling the reality of a writer's lot. Labouring over the next book is only part of it. If a writer is to eat, words must also pay in the interim while a more ambitious project is attempted.

It's not hard to imagine him holding court, *seanchaí* fashion, the metrical rhythms of that distinctive voice rumbling through story after story with scarcely a pause for breath. The oral tradition was alive in him. Imagine having Kiely as your guide: there wouldn't be a street corner or patch of ground but he'd fashion a tale from it, equally likely to be the mock-heroic adventures of a local desperado, or Cúchulainn and his epic doings invoked from the mythic mists. As he says himself in his memoir *Drink to the Bird*, 'This ground is littered with things, cluttered with memories and multiple associations'. He was custodian alike to ancient tales and narratives of recent vintage – just so long as they were good yarns, some of which might even be true. He quotes his father as advising him never to spoil a story for the sake of the truth – the best chronicles tell what should have happened rather than what did.

Whatever you read from his work shares certain common denominators: the tone is scholarly, meditative, expansive and glinting with humour, while plaited through the whole is a passion for Gaelic Ireland. Ever ready to break through are Latin tags or stanzas from poems and songs, for which he had phenomenal recall.

Kiely was of Omagh, even when he was out of it, and the town and its surrounding area permeate his work – characters' names, descriptions, idiosyncrasies and real-life events crop up, thinly disguised, if at all. The speech patterns, too, are recognisably Ulster's. Young men are 'love-deludhered', while one of the townlands is known for inhabitants who are 'an uncivilised crowd of gulpins' – a term still heard regularly, I'm pleased to confirm, along with Dean Swift's 'yahoos', which conveys a similar meaning. But it is Kiely's use of the local topography, above all, which reveals his love for that corner of the globe where he was reared. He was familiar with every nook and cranny. A small lake in the hollow of a bog near New Drumragh Graveyard (where my parents now lie) had 'an almost vocal sadness' about it, he said. Exactly so.

By committing to literature the names of our townlands, he was registering his feelings about them. They were listed with conspicuous delight: Clanabogan, Cavanacaw, Corraduine, Corraheskin. Such poetry in that litany! Group them together, speak them aloud, and they can only be chanted – becoming enchanted. To others, they may be freckles on the national map, never mind the international one, but Kiely treated them with deference as places of worth. And he was right, because it is along byways and not highways that the plain people of Ireland live out their struggles and dreams.

In his stories, those villages, hollows and mountaintops are infused with the memory of an older Ireland which co-exists with the modern version. They are places, he tells us, where folk tales grow as naturally as grass. There, locals walk in the footsteps of legendary figures – history and tradition are not spent forces but living dynamics to Kiely. He wrote a biography of William Carleton, *Poor Scholar*, his research taking him tramping the Clogher Valley where the hedge-schooled writer lived. Kiely defined Carleton as having 'one foot in the traditional Gaelic past', and the same could be said of his biographer.

Just as Joyce calls up real characters in 'The Dead' and bestows immortality on them, Kiely reincarnates his parents, siblings, aunts Kate, Rose and Brigid, neighbours and boyhood companions. People whom the wider world might not consider worthy of a second glance are affectionately realised by Kiely, who values them for their human dignity. Or 'chuman', as he has the local pronunciation render it in several of his short stories.

Omagh people are gratified that a literary man should borrow what we recognised from among ourselves for his work. He used his own life too, as writers generally do, drawing on his abandoned religious vocation and experience of illness in such novels as *Honey Seems Bitter* and *There was an Ancient House* (the title suggested by a line in a poem by Elizabethan poet Edmund Spenser, no friend to Ireland), and the Flann O'Brien-esque *Dogs Enjoy the Morning*. For the latter, I had the privilege of writing an introduction on the occasion of its reissue in 2017, forty-nine years after the initial publication, noting how its storyline sparks with mischief – not least in its goading of the morality police. To my mind, he typed certain sections of that book two-fingered, at least figuratively.

Perhaps locals were slow to tell Kiely they felt a sense of reflected honour from his achievements – *don't be getting above yourself and don't be encouraging others to do it, e'ther* was drilled into every last one of us. But my Omagh was always conscious of Kiely conferring credit on the area. No matter that he lived south of the border, he was out of Omagh. As for the fact that three of his novels were labelled 'in general tendency indecent or obscene' under hard-line censorship laws in the Republic – prohibition showed he mattered. Hadn't he made the censor sit up and take notice? I dare say there were exceptions, but in general people thought no less of him because his novels were banned. Even the strictest Catholics were not immune to a frisson of reflected glory. Certainly, that was the case by the time I became aware of his existence.

As he observed years later when asked about his status as one of a distinguished band of censored writers, 'you did have the feeling that you were with the right people because everybody else was banned that was any damned good'.[1] The banned label was distributed so lavishly, it was almost a disgrace to be excluded. Notorious though the law was, to be scooped up by its dragnet bestowed a certain cachet. Possibly not at the time the sanction was imposed – that must surely have stung, both for writers and their families – but in the aftermath when the extent of the censor's backhanded compliment became apparent.

In recent years, the need to recognise women whose work was submerged by the fledgling Irish State has risen to the fore – women who pushed against the boundaries in the arts, politics, science and other fields. However, Kiely paid attention to a forgotten woman of note as a young man not yet twenty-one years of age. He championed the poet, playwright and journalist Alice Milligan – also out of Omagh – while she still lived and visited her in nearby Mountfield, swinging left on his bicycle into an avenue guarded by fancy gateposts to arrive at an imposing but dilapidated Church of Ireland rectory. That was back in 1940, during the summer he cooled his heels waiting to enrol at University College Dublin. Enthralled, he sat in her smoky drawing room and listened as the 74-year-old slice of living history recounted her memories of a brilliant and imaginative generation of activists and writers. Yeats, Lady Gregory, Maud Gonne, Patrick Pearse and Thomas MacDonagh walked while she spoke. She was, he acknowledged, 'a great woman, neglected by her country and her countrymen'.

It seems likely he was inspired by her, just as he influenced a generation of writers in turn. Anna Burns, who won the 2018 Man Booker Prize for *Milkman*, set in 1970s Belfast, refers to IRA operatives as renouncers, i.e. renouncers of the state. Writing decades earlier in *Nothing Happens in Carmincross*, Kiely calls them destabilisers.

His work in the 1970s ('the bloody 1970s') and 1980s lays bare how intensely offended and angered he was by the killing sprees of the Troubles – guns and bombs were no instruments for problem-solving, in his view, undermining rather than advancing the republican tradition. His novel *Nothing Happens in Carmincross* confronts the North's political violence, as does my favourite work of his, the stand-alone novella *Proxopera*, which Kiely dedicated 'In Memory of the Innocent Dead'. It was published in 1977, reissued in 2015, and prefigures the devastating explosion in Omagh town centre of 1998. In the story, a car bomb is driven into the town by an elderly school teacher whose family has been taken hostage. Its projected location for the explosion mirrors what almost actually happened. In the imaginary account, the bomb is meant for one of Omagh's trademark entry alleyways, between the town hall and the post office. Fiction can supply satisfactory ending which real life often frustrates. What came to pass in Omagh was no less appalling than Kiely envisaged in fiction, but spared his home town. Twenty-one years later, dissident republicans drove a car bomb into Omagh and tried to park it outside the courthouse but were thwarted. Instead, they abandoned the vehicle, complete with lethal cargo, at the bottom of the town and gave a series of confusing warnings. People were evacuated into the path of the blast which killed twenty-nine men, women and children, including a young mother pregnant with twins.

Proxopera is not just prescient but universal, despite the specifics of its setting and timeframe, because it tells of faith, hope and love. Reluctant bomber Granda Binchey remains constant despite the mayhem he is transporting, a combination of ammonium nitrate, gelignite and fuel oil inside a creamery can. 'Ireland, when I hum old songs to myself, is still Ireland through joy and through tears, a most abstract idea, and hope never dies through the long weary years.'

Let us not forget that Kiely worked as a newspaper leader writer for the *Irish Independent* early in his career. Accordingly, it is unsurprising that his first book, *Counties of Contention*, dealt with politics. A study of Ireland's partition, it was published in 1945 and called the border 'that incongruous line that had straggled across the map of Ireland.' I wonder what he'd make of Brexit and its law-of-unintended-consequences impact on 'that amazing sundering and disuniting thing, the Union'? Prophetic here, too, he called for all people of the nation, unionist, nationalist and neither, to find some common ground to face the future 'with hope and energy and infinite charity'. Just twenty-five years after partition, he recognised that reunification could happen only with unionist consent and understood that the challenge was to construct a nation. He was already scrutinising the Irish situation in terms of the wider European context – and time has proven his instinct correct.

By way of a metaphor, in *Counties of Contention* he helped himself to a street in Omagh, a stone's throw from the area where he grew up. On one side of the street stands a terrace of five houses composed of mellowing brick and christened for an Irish saint. Opposite it are five houses plastered with 'sombre cement' and named after an English seaside resort. In his account, the people in the brick terrace considered the cement-capped houses to be grey and Calvinistic, while their inhabitants looked up at the brick row 'and wondered what devilishness or devaleraishness was being plotted there'. Generally, they were civil to one another until the Twelfth of July came around, when the occupants of the houses emerged in their sashes and bowler hats to march behind drums and banners. It was then that the people on the terrace were conscious of disunion, 'of something wider than the width of the street that separated them from their neighbours'. There are devils in details. It was a rift in one small town, noted Kiely, that was every whit as enormous as the one caused by a border with customs posts along both sides of it. Those divisions he characterised as projecting themselves into the spirit.

His Omagh both is and isn't mine. The 'serpentine Shrule' follows the same course through the town today as it did in his youth. Bundoran, where people took daytrips to be awed by the Atlantic, is closer than ever. But I'm a child of the Troubles. He recreates a carefree era when local youths played soccer with the soldiers garrisoned in Omagh and mooched about the barracks, whereas I remember the menacing whirr of helicopters overhead and men in fatigues patrolling with rifles, their faces blacked for camouflage. The world he envisages is prelapsarian.

Yet his world and mine share equivalent points of reference. From time to time, he mentions the town's trademark entries, and they remain in place today: arched alleyways where houses or offices meet overhead, giving access along laneways. When he summons up Knocknamoe Castle, he reminds me of that ballroom of romance (a disco, in point of fact) where I first went dancing as a teenager. It was owned by the Campbells, who had a mighty greyhound named Stockwell Street which competed with honour for the Waterloo Cup. Afterwards, the dog was carried on a platform through the town in a torch-lit procession to a brass-and-reed band accompaniment, Catholics and Protestants alike following and hailing the prodigy. Cheered by this harmony, Kiely's father expressed a view that it might be the will of God for a greyhound to unite Ireland.

'No world is rock-real', Kiely reports a poet telling him, but the worlds he weaves, tapestry fashion, from his memories, experiences and the traditions in which he was steeped from birth are as material as any raconteur can make them. Sometimes, if asked where I'm from, I employ a phrase I encountered for the second time in *Drink to the Bird* – the first time it was drilled into me in Irish class at Loreto Convent. '*As an Ómaigh mé*, out of Omagh me; I'm from Omagh.' Perhaps he was tickled by its double meaning – where he sprang from but never left completely. Out of, for now. Destined to return. As he did, because he lies in the town's Dublin Road cemetery.

When I speak the words I remember him standing there on hilly High Street, absorbing the scene while he nods at neighbours and schoolfellows – a man who made it appear possible that anyone could write if only they had the courage to lift their pen and begin. Continuity, as Kiely himself would say. Probably with an anecdote thrown in.

GERALD DAWE

•

An Unfortunate Country: Reading Benedict Kiely's *Poor Scholar*, 1974–2018

I

The car we were in was a Mini. 'You look like de Valera with those glasses on. Whatever happens, I'll speak, not you.' I was handing in my dissertation on William Carleton during the worst days of the Ulster Workers' Council strike in May 1974 and was being driven by my stepfather to what was then called the New University of Ulster[1] outside Coleraine. To get there, we needed petrol and so we stopped at a station on the Upper Newtownards Road in Belfast. The Ulster Defence Association had control of the pumps. A man in a balaclava stood listening to our request and the extenuating circumstances, and we got the petrol, though not before he had looked at my student ID and eyed me up and down. Then, patting the roof of the Mini, waved us on, wishing me the best of luck.

The road wound its way through silent towns and townlands and as we reached the security of Tower Block 2 of NUU, I slipped out of the car, straightened up and dashed to the departmental office, submitting my dissertation in the nick of time. And then we returned to Belfast; an eerie, unforgettable journey that, for some reason I cannot recall, made me think of John Le Carré's novel *The Spy Who Came in from the Cold*.

Alan Warner, my supervisor at NUU, and Brendan Kennelly of Trinity College, Dublin, the external examiner, met midway in Ballymascanlon House Hotel in Dundalk, to adjudicate on the various dissertations of that year and, before I knew it, I had the examination over and was hanging out in Belfast wondering what was next. Working in the Fine Arts Department of the Central Library, as it happened, for a few months before, the best of all good luck, an application to continue working on William Carleton took me off, thanks to a Major State Award, to the West of Ireland and University College, Galway, where Lorna Reynolds, the Professor of English, would – on Alan Warner's recommendation – take me on as supervisor for my graduate thesis: *William Carleton: Novelist or Social Historian*.

In those late months of 1974 and into 1975, the 'Troubles' were entering a fatal downward spiral.[2] Galway seemed beyond it all, though my returns home to Belfast were indescribable reminders of just how brutal things actually were, with the sectarian murder of a young poet acquaintance and the fearfulness of bombings in pubs and shops, recounted in detail by, among others, my mother, who was still working at the time in the city centre. I wrote letters to the handful of Carleton experts, older writers, including Benedict Kiely, Thomas Flanagan and Anthony Cronin,[3] as well as to the enterprising founder-editor of the US-based *Carleton Newsletter*, Eileen Sullivan Ibarra, and waded my way through Carleton's, at times, heavy-set prose style, sentimentality and moralising. Outside of Flanagan's thoughtful critical overview of nineteenth-century Irish novelists,[4] and scattered essays here and there from, among others, Patrick Kavanagh,[5] and random pieces by W.B. Yeats,[6] Carleton existed on the margins of what was still called 'Anglo-Irish literature'.

While I had kept from my earlier undergraduate research various books on Irish folklore, Irish language literature, several histories of nineteenth-century Ireland and travel books written by English and continental travellers, the one study that proved priceless was Benedict Kiely's *Poor Scholar: A Study of the Works and Days of William Carleton (1794–1869)*, originally published in London by Sheed and Ward in 1947[7] and featuring John Joseph Slattery's portrait of Carleton in the possession of the National Gallery of Ireland.

The copy of *Poor Scholar* I possessed back then was a paperback, published in Dublin by The Talbot Press in 1972, but in front of me today is the original hardback, bought, according to the signature within, by Malachy A. Conlon in February 1948. Seventy years on, Kiely's book stands the test of time in its ability to convey, like an expressionist painting, the ferocity of the conditions out of which William Carleton emerged and the contradictions of being viewed as a representative of the Irish peasant class, with its bilingual culture and literary amplitude and its imperilled way of life, along with its traditional strengths.

It is an apocalyptic story and no one can read of Carleton's journey, as narrated by Kiely, without being deeply moved by both the drive and by the huge economic challenges and social obstacles that were placed in the way of any advancement. Carleton's life story reveals a world that present-day Ireland is reluctant to revisit. Yet in its dramatic difference it underscores the extraordinary distance the country had travelled in a relatively short period of time – from the unimaginable conditions of the Great Famine of 1845–49 – Carleton's greatest novel, *The Black Prophet* (1846), draws upon earlier famines in 1817 and 1822 – to the declaration a century later of the Irish Republic in 1948, shortly after Kiely's study was published.

II

Poor Scholar is remarkable for its own writing, though, and Kiely's ability to revisit the language of early nineteenth-century Ulster. There is a kind of infuriated instability at the heart of the English which shifts from a high-toned 'literary' voice, somewhat formalised and inflected with classical learning and mid-century English piety, to the syntactically unmoored energies of speech rendered in all its vernacular shifts:

> Taking his place in the tattered circle the boy [Carleton] was beginning something that was to absorb much of his energy, much of his time: a hungry search for wisdom, a joy in mere verbiage right up to his ecstasy … in strutting about the country uttering sesquipedalian[8] words. (24)

Is this language-consciousness an inheritance from the Tyrone-Armagh-Fermanagh counties of Ulster and the intimate influences of Gaelic song and story, alongside the pulse of classically infused Hedge Schools? Certainly, in Kiely's reading of Carleton there is a family feeling in the writing which would be identified in the decades after his book appeared by an international readership of the kind Carleton had long desired. Is there any likelihood of there being a tradition based around the geography of south Ulster which embraces such voices as Flann O'Brien, Patrick McCabe, Dermot Healy, Paul Muldoon and Jan Carson? Kiely's study is unconcerned with such possibilities. In his reading, Carleton Country is an unfortunate country and *Poor Scholar* is a guide to the terrain:

> He was born into an unfortunate country at a terrible chaotic time, and on that wintry night he had come up against one of the things that made the country unfortunate: bigotry, bitterness, the neighbour crossing your threshold in his yeoman's uniform, with his gun and prodding bayonet. (13)

Poor Scholar as literary anthropology renders the contradictions of an Ireland in which, for instance, the Priest is identified through 'the long association in suffering' with the People, and the People, as Kiely quotes Carleton's introduction to *Tales of Ireland* (1834), are 'unknown' and misrepresented:

> I found them, a class unknown in literature, unknown by their own landlords, and unknown by those in whose hands much of their destiny was placed. If I became the historian of their habits and manners, their

feelings, their prejudices, their superstitions and their crimes; if I have attempted to delineate their moral, religious and physical state, it was because I saw no person willing to undertake a task which surely must be looked upon as an important one ... I was anxious that those who ought, but did not, understand their character, should know them, not merely for selfish purposes, but that they should teach them to know themselves and appreciate their rights, both moral and civil, as rational men, who owe obedience to law, without the necessity of being slave either to priest or landlord. (45)

There is also in Kiely's narrative an assumption of the positive role of religion for the unhoused, famine-stricken masses as the apocalyptic image of famine overshadows his study:

And all the time the Irish people were dying miserably in cabins that stank to the skies with fever and the stench of putrid bodies, or dying in ditches or on the desolate roads when the landlord's crowbar men had battered the cabins level with the ground, or passing out through the seaports on their way to new lands. (123)

The contrasts come from Carleton's (and Kiely's) love of landscape, books and literature of all kinds, with particularly moving anecdotes about Carleton's discovery of Defoe, Burns, Lesage's *Gil Blas*, some wonderful comparisons with Turgenev and, when Carleton makes his final move to Dublin, Dickens:

> Those first years of life in Dublin must have given [Carleton] for his own forever the secrets of the streets of Dublin as Dickens was given in his boyhood the secret of the incredible world that is the streets of London. But Dickens was at home in London ... Carleton was never at home in Dublin. (59)

And with James Joyce:

> James Joyce had been at home in Dublin, happy and unhappy in Dublin. Dublin was in his bones. In Paris or in Trieste he sat down to write, and remembered Dublin. William Carleton did his writing where Joyce had left his heart. But he looked back across flat land to the valley where the grass was more green and the sunshine more golden than anywhere else in the wide world. He saw also a thousand valleys and a thousand hill-slopes, bare places on mountains, flat land along rivers, stony places by the sea. Everywhere he saw his people, eight millions of them on one small island. Above them the sky was blackening with the darkness of doom. (60)

The idyll is suddenly brought up short by the statistical reality-check in much the same way as the young Carleton's shock on entering Dirty Lane, in the inner city, is put centre-stage in Kiely's account; an experience and setting which reminds one of the tragic end of James Clarence Mangan's short life or of the life of Rashers in James Plunkett's social realist novel *Strumpet City*.[9] Drawing on Carleton's *Autobiography*, Kiely paints a dreadful scene:

Going down the steps to the cellar in Dirty Lane he lost for the moment that vision. On shakedowns of straw with sheets of rag, men and women in various degrees of drink lay asleep. By the light of a red fire he saw the lame, the blind, the dumb, broken and diseased people. He saw also those who, during the day and for business purposes, had assumed all the infirmities of the flesh ... Those who were still awake sang and chatted and shouted slang, and the lad from the green country felt for the first time the creeping touch of a leprous obscenity. (62)

III

Even with the achievement of a solid literary reputation, largely based in Ireland, but recognised in Britain too with his books being published in London, Edinburgh and Belfast, Carleton struggled financially for most of his life. As Kiely remarks:

Later on, Carleton lived in a prosperous part of the south side of the city. He became a familiar figure in Dublin, but he never really mixed in society, never held the place among urban people that he had once held among the simple people of the Clogher valley. (122)

A not unknown condition when one considers the distortions of self which twentieth-century figures such as Patrick Kavanagh went through, even though most of their adult lives were lived in the city. Kiely, the Omagh writer, had an obvious sympathy: 'William Carleton was a peasant who became a novelist and did his best to be a reformer.' (145)

And it is this sense of being a 'reformer', the social agenda that Carleton took on in an effort to reformulate the political and cultural prejudices of the British administration and its Irish counterparts – the landlord system, the wasted economy, the flood of emigration, the imperialism of the time – that led to his (and Kiely's?) version of a pragmatic nationalism; nothing like the high romantic idealism that Yeats would promote in the generation after Carleton's death in 1869.

Kiely's reading of Carleton's condition has a magisterial inner logic to it that he would revisit in his own fiction-making, such as the powerful novella *Proxopera* (1977), subtitled 'A Tale of Modern Ireland':

> In no other country could a man writing to interpret a people be faced so terribly with the task of interpreting what looked like the total extinction of the people. A writer could hardly feel that his work would go to found or strengthen a distinctive literary tradition; and when the smell of death became too strong and the only colour in the world was the denial of all colour, the creative artist could do little more than record atrocity after atrocity, writing pamphlet material that has value today because of the merciless character of its realism. (156)

The experience of violence such as that recounted in his story 'Wildgoose Lodge' and the trauma of witnessing dead bodies hanging on gallows never left Carleton, notwithstanding the succour of a strong and loving wife, Jane, and family, and latterly the financial support of a civil list pension. Violence, however, was endemic in Irish society, as Kiely points out:

> [Carleton] could never, like [John] Mitchel, the gentleman who became a revolutionary, welcome murder as a weapon against murder, and disorder from below as the only answer to disorder imposed from above. In that he was very much less logical than Mitchel and the whole revolutionary Ireland and revolutionary Europe of which Mitchel was a part. (145)

Alluding in passing to Arthur Koestler's novel *Darkness at Noon* (1940)[10] and the pitiless manner in which the 'logical revolutionary ... accepts the necessity of violence as a weapon against violence', Kiely makes a crucial distinction about Carleton's humanity. The terrible cost, post-famine, is captured in an unforgettable extract from a letter to Carleton from his friend William Frederick Wakeman, a teacher of drawing at Portora Royal School, Enniskillen, describing a walking tour through County Tyrone:

> This part of the country must be greatly changed from what you will recollect of it. *All* the young people appear to have emigrated. The land is almost entirely under grass. Yesterday I had a glorious walk from this town through Derrygonnelly to Knockmore, and home by the shore of Lough Erne. In that march of about

twenty-two miles I did not see more than eight people. (170)

Kiely's Carleton had

> lived a quiet life, the quietude disturbed only by adventures of the literary man, by enthusiasms for new ideas, by occasional and transient enmities for other literary people, by quarrels with publishers, by meeting different people, intensely interesting as real people always are to the creative artist making his own world out of what his eyes see and his mind imagines of the world around him. (122)

It was as if Kiely had in *Poor Scholar* transformed William Carleton, the writer from Prillisk, near Clogher, County Tyrone, into a contemporary of 1940s Dublin, while the cataclysm of the Great Famine can be read as a metaphor for the Holocaust.

Along with Kiely's other volumes of critical non-fiction – *Counties of Contention* (1945)[11] and *Modern Irish Fiction: A Critique* (1950)[12] – *Poor Scholar* awaits a new readership. Thinking back to those first encounters with William Carleton and Kiely's animated retelling of his life and times, there is a remarkable consistency, in literary, intellectual and cultural terms, to Benedict Kiely's writing, possibly obscured by his one-time, much better-known public persona and manner as a broadcaster and man about town. Behind that mask, as these three studies reveal, there was a deeply concerned, serious and extraordinarily well-read artist who both loved his country passionately but who also knew by heart its failings and contradictions and had the self-confidence to spell these out for his fellow citizens at home and farther afield, wherever work took him. Kiely, like others of his generation now somewhat out of fashion – Mary Lavin and Aidan Higgins, for instance – had a vision of Ireland that was often tragic or acerbic or both, but yet was filled with the gloriously anarchic energies of the imagination as well as a discriminating intelligence and knowledge of the world.

DEREK HAND

•

Benedict Kiely and the 1950s: The Struggle to be Modern

In his critical study of modern Irish fiction, *Modern Irish Fiction: A Critique* (1950), Benedict Kiely argued that after the Irish War of Independence and the subsequent civil war, 'The time for heroic gesture was over and the future must be as prosaic as building a wall.'[1] Certainly a pervading sense of a benighted Irish world devoid of innovation and energy,[2] of Irish identity reduced to narrow, preordained categories,[3] feeds into a notion of Irish writing itself being narrow and wanting. Seán O'Faoláin suggested that Irish life was numbingly humdrum and the consequence for the would-be Irish fiction writer was imaginative deflation:

> Our sins are tawdry, our virtues childlike, our revolts desultory and brief, our submissions formal and frequent. In Ireland a policeman's lot is a supremely happy one. God smiles, the priest beams, and the novelist groans.[4]

And yet, rebuking O'Faoláin's thesis, Kiely's critical survey attests that novels were being written in Ireland after the heroic age of the revival period and that, indeed, it was the novel that was best suited to mark out this new post-independence territory, giving voice to the stories of the ordinary life of women and men as it was being lived.[5]

It is interesting to explore Kiely's own fiction at this moment as both a response to and a critique of the general state of Irish fiction. As well as this critical analysis of the novel and short story, Kiely had already written a history of partition, *Counties of Contention*, and *Poor Scholar*, a study of William Carleton. On one level he is acknowledging a time of transition between the past and the present as he takes ownership of his cultural and political heritage in both these books, surveying the scene and staking his claim not just to that past but, more importantly, to the future. With regard to these beginnings as well as to his immediate literary contemporaries, he was also acutely aware of the need to carve out a space for his own art and vision. It has usually been argued that the 1940s and 1950s were a time of benighted trauma, a dark place to be escaped from, and O'Faoláin's argument reflects this. It might equally be argued, though, that in relation to the novel form in particular, there was a diversity of stories being heard and that this was actually a very productive moment in the literary history of Ireland.[6]

A brief glance at some of the work of this period confirms this. Elizabeth Bowen's *The World of Love* (1955), for instance, follows the well-known contours of the Big House novel, but actually offers a troubling depiction of stunted development in modern Ireland. Mary Lavin in *Mary O'Grady* (1950) and Brian Moore in *The*

Lonely Passion of Judith Hearne (1955) portray the still-powerful Catholic Church's grip on the Irish imagination. The rural world of the small farmer in Patrick Kavanagh's novel *Tarry Flynn* (1948) is presented as a stifling place, not so much in thrall to the morals of the Catholic Church but to the self-policing community itself, with its withering and unforgiving suspicion of difference. While Kavanagh exploited the comic potential of his characters, Sam Hanna Bell's *December Bride* (1951) renders how insular and isolated country life can actually be and how speech itself becomes truncated and limited in the sectarian Ulster world of inherent and inherited mistrust. The semi-autobiographical *Borstal Boy* (1958) by Brendan Behan exploded onto the literary scene, its linguistic flair and energy, political engagement and up-to-date social conscience giving a polite readership access to a whiff of sulphur.

Within this context, Benedict Kiely in *The Cards of the Gambler* (1953) and *There was an Ancient House* (1955) represents an interesting counterpoint, mapping the emergence of the empowered Irish middle-classes.[7] Class is central to his vision of contemporary Ireland, and his work is endlessly open to the subtle, undeclared class codes within Irish society that separate country from town, farmer from civil servant. Kiely recognises, at a very practical level, that the undercurrent of desire and aspiration – the all-consuming struggle for political and cultural independence that coloured the previous generation's artistic endeavour – was no longer appropriate. So, despite the presence of partition and the still persistent realities of the processes of decolonisation on the political and cultural level, his fictional world is one of relative containment and calm.

In his first two novels, *Land Without Stars* (1946) and *In a Harbour Green* (1949), despite being set in and around Omagh in Northern Ireland and using the backdrop of the Second World War and local IRA engagements, the atmosphere is one of quiet, untroubled existence. Rather than politics or religion, the emphasis is on the individual's growth into maturity through the Joycean filters of sexuality, morality and intellectual development. Indeed, in relation to what would happen in the late 1960s when the tension within the North erupted into violence, for Kiely it is not religion that divides people; rather, it is class that keeps communities apart. Also absent are any of the linguistic anxieties on display in the work of either Elizabeth Bowen or, indeed, Samuel Beckett in his contemporaneous *Trilogy* (1955–8). Neither is Kiely concerned with testing the form of the novel as a means of expression in the ways that James Joyce or Flann O'Brien had done. Instead, he is eager to shift the reader's attention on to the stories being told, the poise of his prose and his formal control giving perfect expression to the nature of the modern lives under scrutiny.

The rewards of such a manoeuvre are many. Dramatist Brian Friel acknowledged this in an early review of *The Cards of the Gambler*:

> Not only is [it] Benedict Kiely's best novel but it is one of the finest novels that has been written in this country in years. It will certainly sweep away such niggardly epithets as 'promising' and 'regional' and raise the author to the position he deserves.[8]

To transcend the local and enter into the realm of the universal, to consider not just the exceptional circumstance of the Irish scene but connect with common human concerns, is what is required. *The Cards of the Gambler*, in an overtly conscious way, certainly attempts to do just that. The author deliberately refuses to name the city of Dublin at the outset, preferring instead to render the urban and suburban streets anonymously. What is most immediately notable is how the novel moves away from the serene naturalism of his earlier work as he ventures into the realm of the fantastic and the magical. Kiely weaves together the traditional Irish folk tale of the gambler who makes a pact with the devil and the European Faust theme, and sets it in the present day.

The unnamed hero, a doctor and a gambler, is presented in the opening pages as having lost everything in a game of cards. Without a reputation and without money, he stumbles upon Death in priestly garb in a pub who introduces him to God. The gambler makes a deal with the latter so that he may never lose at cards again. Kiely brilliantly juxtaposes the mundane rituals of suburban life with the fantastic and makes his hero's dilemma accessible and believable. The focus on gambling is of interest in a modern context: gambling gives access to a momentary negation of rules and regulations, allowing the individual to embrace the possibilities of chance. And yet, any gambler is, as Walter Benjamin argues, 'driven by essentially narcissistic and aggressive desires for omnipotence'.[9] Indeed, reinforcing this, Kiely's gambler has a second wish granted by God: to be able to heal all his patients. Benjamin develops his argument by suggesting there is a link between erotic desire and the pleasure of winning, meaning that gambling becomes a pre-eminent signifier of the bourgeois imagination, as it is an expression of that which must be denied.[10] Thus, the gambler is the quintessential middle-class figure, his encounter and pact with God and Death leading not only to existential musings on his part, but also directing him towards attaining what anyone of his class would hope for, a solid reputation and wealth.

The interweaving of the Irish folktale with the contemporary story gives the novel a plot of sorts in that much of the action revolves round the tricksterish relationship between the gambler and Death, with the gambler inevitably paying the price of his deal with the lives of his lover and his son. More relevant, perhaps, is the portrait of the gambler's modern, if not modernist, ennui. Even in the opening pages, confronted with the loss of everything, the gambler seems curiously calm and unmoved. His wish always to win at cards negates the purpose of the gambling in that it neutralises this channel for excitement, doing away with the chance to transcend the numbing tedium and monotony of the everyday. One consequence is that the gambler lacks agency, simply reacting to events and situations. His pact has robbed him of experience instead of enhancing it, and thus his actual experience is further deadened. The ennui experienced by the hero is a deep and self-perpetuating one, a general malaise of dissoluteness that cannot be overcome.

Kiely offers a remarkably sustained portrait of one of the main challenges of modernity – the demand on the individual to discover, or create, a self or identity, and the burdensome consequences of that need. Although the gambler might have achieved his heart's desire, in doing so he loses access to the world of feeling and the world of companionship. His, then, is a thoroughly modern dilemma. And when the gambler finally dies and enters into the afterlife, comically and brilliantly presented as a clean and well-lit airport, Death imparts to him the knowledge that '"Your hell, I'm sure, would be shaped like a respectable suburb".' The gambler then imagines such a place which, in truth, seems like the perfect setting for a modern novel: small lives, petty jealousies and humdrum victories. As an astute early reviewer of the novel cautioned:

> Mr. Kiely will write an outstanding book when he realises that it must not necessarily be the sort of book that pious people in respectable suburbs feel they must be careful about.[11]

The twist in the tale is that the hero loses that which he had thought he most despised in life: the commonplace comforts of home and access to a suburbia which, while respectable on the surface, is a potential melting pot of malevolence beneath.

By setting up a correspondence between an ancient folk story and a modern setting, *The Cards of the Gambler* critiques Catholicism at an angle quite different to the more direct challenges in the *non serviam* Joycean mode. Kiely's is a more measured, less confrontational approach, highlighting the incongruity of the demands of the modern individual, who ought to be the measure of all things, and the demands of a religion that puts all power and authority into a transcendent being. Can both 'ideas' coexist? Here they can, owing in part, I would argue, to the deployment of the folktale, which at the level of form and genre gestures towards a universal notion of the transcendent which is not linked to any one faith. It might also be said, though, that placing God and Death in the all-too-human realm robs them of any mystery. Death, especially, appears driven by very human desires rather than the divine. His is also, in a way, an oddly bureaucratic job, with rules and regulations to be followed, boxes to be ticked and targets to be met.

Kiely's next novel, *There was an Ancient House*, is more direct in its analysis of the Catholic Church in Ireland in the 1940s and 1950s. It is based on his own experience when he went to the Jesuit novitiate in Emo Park, County Laois, for a year in 1937/38. Two novices are the main focus. MacKenna, a young man from a small town in Northern Ireland, is an artist figure, and the older Barragry is a worldly-wise and world-weary journalist. Together both represent perhaps the two aspects of Kiely's own personality. With 'stylistic restraint' the author perceives that the ills of religious life spring from these eager, energetic and spiritually idealistic young men being forced to live apart from the world.[12] The walls surrounding the ancient house are there to keep them in, but they serve to keep the world out: 'the barrier of the demesne wall, the house and its way followed them, cut them off from the people they met on the roads'.

The atmosphere of the novitiate resembles that of the Big House environment of Elizabeth Bowen, Somerville and Ross and Molly Keane, with the community of novices bound to rituals set down by generations past that they must internalise and make their own. Kiely must have been aware of the disturbing allusions to colonial violence and Ireland's colonial history in making use of Spenser's *The Faerie Queen* to give the novel its title, though he does not overtly make that connection for his readers. Perhaps it is up to readers themselves to ponder the link between the civilising presence of a house that brings 'good and godly deeds' and that culture on which it imposes itself. Certainly the narrator signals the dissipation of the older Anglo-Irish owners of the house, telling of how the religious order had taken over the dilapidated home: 'That unholy growth out of foundational darkness ... symbolised decay, days gone in drink and dice ...' They restored what had been, bringing a new sense of order and civilisation to the place.

And yet the tension for both Barragry and MacKenna, in Yeatsian fashion, comes not from 'the quarrel with others' but from 'the quarrel with themselves'.[13] Again, both men wrestle with the realities of this stark division between the world within and the world without, in the end recognising that they are separated from the flock they are meant to serve. That realm of life, of experience and of existence – the fallen world inhabited by their fellow women and men – is not their world. Throughout the novel the divergence between these two realities is made clear. What marks off the novitiate world from the world outside the demesne walls is an absence of colour. The former is 'a white world ... All the whiteness made him afraid. Was it black or white was the absence of colour?' The novel ends in an appreciation of a world of glorious colour: 'This world was a multi-coloured arc. It was black and white, blue and white, grey and white, blue and red'.

In truth, these young men are forced to have a foot in the otherworld well before their time: 'He walked on. No use in standing like a ghost looking enviously at men still alive.' It is clear where life in all its forms is to be found.

MacKenna, like Joyce's Stephen Dedalus before him, transfers his religious sensibility into the realm of art. It is said of him that he possesses a penchant for the 'apt quotation' for every situation and eventuality. The work is littered with reference to and quotations from an array of writers such as Lord Macaulay, Alfred Noyes, Joris-Karl Huysmans and Douglas Hyde, as well as snippets from street ballads and prayers. This is a highly textualised world, and it is the way that MacKenna sees the world and interacts with it. Experience and even the landscape are overlain with texts, connecting the present with the past, and bringing meaning and significance to everyday reality.

What it interesting about this, and indeed Kiely's own delightful 'predilection for quotations',[14] is how it articulates precisely the nature of his art at this juncture and the ways in which it inhabits the Irish post-revolutionary space. Joyce's writing, and particularly *Ulysses*, gave expression to a modernist disquiet with not just language but with enlightenment knowledge itself, as he dismantled the modes of the realist novel and challenged the authority embedded in traditional forms. For Joyce's fictional alter ego Stephen Dedalus, this meant that all his undergraduate knowledge, captured brilliantly in, for instance, the opening paragraphs of the 'Proteus' episode on Sandymount Strand, is a burden and a barrier to his fully experiencing the now. If history (Irish included) is for Dedalus 'a nightmare from which I am trying to awake',[15] so too then is all that literary and cultural baggage that stands in the way of his creativity in the present moment. But for Kiely and his characters in *There was an Ancient House*, knowledge and learning are self-evidently good, connecting the novices to the past in a productive way. For MacKenna, his storehouse of references and quotations are not 'fragments ... shored up against [his] ruins';[16] rather they are palpable signifiers of his place in the world, bringing him closer to it, making him an integral part of it. Knowledge and learning are to be valued because they bring confidence, and because they also become an act of imaginative possession.

Three of Barragry's friends from his past life journey to the locale of the house, one of them his old girlfriend. They do not meet, but the girl takes a swim in the lake by the house, supposedly the scene that led to the temporary banning of the novel by the Censorship Board. While these friends abandon themselves to the luxuries of a freedom seldom enjoyed by those who dwell in the novitiate, their existence seems somewhat disconnected and aimless, empty, in comparison. Thus, one purpose of the novel is to rejoice in this enclosed world rather than to disparage or mock it. In the end, even though both MacKenna and Barragry leave the house, the religious life is transfigured rather than wholly abandoned.

While Kiely sees faults and offers criticism of this Catholic institution, he does not, nor does he want to, jeopardise the status quo. Emphasising this is his deployment of a gentle, relaxed and controlled realism which manifests no anxiety. This novel celebrates the liberal bourgeois trait of tolerance, even in those moments when the author's perspective wryly bursts pretension and pomposity. His is certainly akin to

Joyce in that he is not above making fun of the various versions of himself in the novel. He suggests in his critique of modern Irish fiction that his own moment is one where the novel and the novelist is caught between the desire for rejection and acceptance.[17] Kiely's position of being part of the establishment and also wanting to be at an angle to it in order to create vital art is ultimately a precarious one.

In a moment of self-reflexivity, Barragry wonders about writing a novel of his experiences in the novitiate:

> When I get back into the world I'll write a novel about this place: the lake and the trees, the seclusion from everything, even newspapers, the prayer, the charity, the peace, the blues, the noonday devil, the fear for perseverance ...

It could be said that what is truly attractive about the house and the religious order are the rituals to be undertaken which, despite being of the older world, actually open up a space for self-reflection and examination. In Joycean fashion, then, it is the past that leads to the future, tradition which underpins true modernity.

In these novels, Benedict Kiely focuses on the concerns of the Irish middle classes, those who inhabit the realities of the post-revolutionary period, those who eschew the heroic gesture in favour of more routine tasks. One of his achievements is to make the characters our contemporaries rather than simply representatives of a particular historical time. With formal poise and intellectual sophistication, he presents characters who have a stake in the new emerging nation in ways, perhaps, that the previous generation could not. If the struggle of that earlier generation was communal and national, bound up with history and politics, then the struggle for this generation was to craft an identity that was true to its own contexts and pressures. Writers too, in turn, had to be true to that new moment and to the realities of life as it was being lived, and to offer other narratives and intimate histories that had been overlooked or silenced. In an estimation of this period in Irish art and culture, Brian Fallon has said that '[i]t was not a golden age' but that there were occasional 'seams of gold'.[18] Benedict Kiely's work offers us one glimpse of some of that precious metal in the sparkling reflection of which we may see and appreciate the struggle towards modernity.

PATRICIA CRAIG

•

'He Could Recite All Night':
An Appreciation of Benedict Kiely

The first thing you notice about Benedict Kiely's writing is its exuberance, its relish for allusion and high colour and hyperbole. Kiely has all the *seanchaí*'s feeling for extravagance, tempered, in his case, by a sardonic undertone. His marvellous stories are a repository of decoration and delectation. They come replete with the utmost susceptibility to sensation, and all manner of embellishment. They are grounded, indeed, in acute observation of the world around him, but the everyday encounters or experiences that impinge on his consciousness are freighted with the stuff of myth. Take the early story 'The Heroes in the Dark House', in which an old collector of Gaelic folk tales, Mr Broderick, 'found it hard to separate the people in the tales from the people who told them'. And, adding a further layer of reference, the legendary heroes are fused in the old man's mind with the heroes of the United States Army (briefly garrisoned during the Second World War at Knocknashee in County Tyrone), and with the heroes of the Irish uprising of 1798, when pikes were forged and sedition fostered in the stone-floored kitchens of rebel houses. Mr Broderick, like his creator, is not attracted to understatement. '"There was never a departure like it since the world was made,"' he declares, following the exodus of American troops. '"They were gone," he said, '"like snow off a ditch."' This is the way the local legend begins to crystallise. In the right hands, the scope for aggrandizement is unlimited – or, as Kiely put it himself in an *Irish Times* interview in 1982: 'There do seem to be an enormous number of things going on all the time, and all that is good.'

Benedict Kiely had his own way of telling a story, however much he's indebted to traditional button-holing tactics, and to vast areas of local lore. Rapid shifts of emphasis, odd angles of vision, rag-bag impressions, all contribute to Kiely's distinctive method, a method that enables him to wander freely and embellish extensively. At the same time, a high degree of control and high pressure are maintained throughout his narratives. Kiely goes at things full tilt, like the two sides in the annual re-enactment of the Battle of the Boyne at Scarva in County Down, which makes a presiding emblem for his story 'Mock Battle'.

This story contains a number of typical Kiely components: a journey, a local event, an edgy relationship between a husband and wife, some characters endowed with strong traits, a lot of borrowed phrases and catchphrases, an incident or two remembered from an earlier time. What happens? A newspaper reporter based in Dublin has come north on the train, accompanied by his wife, to be met by a photographer and driven to the scene of the celebratory skirmish. The reporter's wife keeps needling him about his friendship with a tennis player named Alison, a bouncing girl. Other bouncing girls are frequently to be encountered in Kiely's pages, some with peculiar names like Maruna, and one is identified only by the clothes she is wearing: jodhpurs. Some, like the red-haired Gobnait in the singularly entitled 'Your Left Foot is Crazy' in *A Letter to Peachtree* (1987), are glorious girls out of the distant past: forty, fifty years or more ago.

The vanished girls are evoked with admiration. The backward look is strongly developed in Benedict Kiely's universe. The past is filled with monumental goings-on. In 'A Letter to Peachtree', for instance, the eponymous epistle is the work of a research student called Karney, over from America to study the novels of Brinsley MacNamara. He is writing to a woman of his acquaintance back in Atlanta, Georgia, and to entertain her – and us – he comes up with a full-blown Irish escapade of the 1940s or 1950s, complete with train journey, parochial hall, quaint Catholicism, incest, drink in large quantities, literary tit-bits, valiant ladies, mountain roads, late-night conviviality and all. The atmosphere of this piece is overwhelming, but Kiely keeps it under control – just – by treating it as a kind of indigenous burlesque. He is adept at exercising his feelings for oddity and inflation, and his central theme is often approached by way of some rocky by-road. By-roads and by-words alike appeal to him. Over-the-top doings in out-of-the-way places form his stock-in-trade, but a knowing, sardonic approach to his material, combined with prodigious expertise, keeps him aligned to a contemporary creativity.

If the misbehaviour of a bullock on a fair day is enough to set his imagination going, and going full-bloodedly, he can also surprise us with a story about a molester whose trick is to spray paint at girls in their good clothes ('Through the Fields in Gloves'). Another story, 'Secondary Top', has at its centre a schoolteacher whose behaviour towards the young girls in his charge isn't absolutely impeccable; letters of complaint signed 'Worried Mother' begin to reach the school. Two flippant detectives, passing themselves off as fishermen, arrive to sort things out. Kiely's own resolutions are sometimes as haphazard as the contretemps that precede them.

Locality is important, especially as it relates to Kiely's childhood surroundings, and in particular Omagh – 'Sweet Omagh Town', as the popular song has it. Kiely remained all his life under the spell of the place-names of County Tyrone: old Drumragh and Cassiebawn and Claramore and Mullagharn.

> ... townlands like Corraheskin, Drumlish, Cornavara, Dooish, The Minnieburns and Claramore, and small towns like Drumquin and Dromore were all within a ten-mile radius of our town and something of moment or something amusing had happened in every one of them.

So says the narrator of 'A Journey to the Seven Streams'. Something of moment or something amusing: it's as good a summing-up as any of Kiely's modus operandi. This particular story, recounted in retrospect, takes on a symbolic character that overlies the remembered family excursion in a ramshackle car (a car, indeed, that fixes in its final and most extreme form the character of *being* ramshackle); and the story ends on a sombre note, with a funeral cortege retracing the route of the glorious outing. A framework of anecdote, association and illumination enables Kiely to formalise nostalgia, thereby diminishing its sentimental content. 'In memory glorified', as Yeats has it, perhaps, but not prettified.

Among the outstanding old people of Kiely's fabulous childhood are John and Thady O'Neill, or their originals, in 'Homes on the Mountain', who live in the kind of exorbitant disorder encapsulated by W.F. Marshall in his best-known lines:

> The deil a man in this townlan'
> Was claner rared nor me,
> But I'm livin' in Drumlister
> In clabber to the knee.

'Clabber to the knee' evokes precisely the state of Kiely's domestically incompetent but hearty old brothers whose sagging farmhouse is in pointed contrast to a new home erected nearby at the whim of a returned American ('There wasn't a building job like it since the building of the Tower of Babel') – a returned American intent on re-creating his barefoot boyhood, or an upgraded version of it. Nothing, indeed, but the pressure of some fearful, bemusing nostalgia, the narrator's mother thinks, could have led this (unnamed) character to exchange the comforts of Philadelphia for the bleak wet side of Dooish Mountain.

'Homes on the Mountain' treats different varieties of make-believe, dilapidation and pusillanimity (the old bachelor brother who courted a girl for sixty years and let her die a virgin), all common and deplorable Irish states, if now well and truly in the past, and suggested here by Kiely with not the least tinge of sourness. The only comment, and it's unspoken, is in the words of certain facile songs which beguiled the narrator at the age of twelve: 'When I lived in Sweet Ballinacrazy, dear, the girls were all bright as a daisy, dear.'

It was Elizabeth Bowen who cited the sexlessness of Irish writing (as long ago as 1946, it's true; things have dramatically changed in this respect over the last fifty-odd years). I don't think anything in Benedict Kiely's stories, for all their vigour and occasional outspokenness, would cause her to revise that opinion. For Kiely, the sexual act is best portrayed as a feat, like weight-lifting or horse-breaking. As 'Homes on the Mountain' has it, '"There was the day ... when Martin Murphy and myself looked over a whin hedge at yourself and Molly Quigley from Crooked Bridge making love in a field. Between you, you ruined a half-acre of turnips."' Even Kiely's Madame Butterfly, the Dublin prostitute who is as artlessly carnal as Molly Bloom, carries no erotic charge whatever. (The story in which she appears, 'A Ball of Malt and Madame Butterfly', is shot through with lines from Yeats and Synge: Kiely at his creative borrowing again.) Neither does Pascal Stakelum, 'the notorious rural rake' in 'A Great God's Angel Standing'. In Kiely's world, priests and rural rakes aren't barred from being on the best of terms with one another; and because of his friendship with Father Paul, Pascal is himself mistaken for a priest and forced to hear the confession of a lunatic in an asylum. (Kiely's stories often follow unexpected and breathtaking lines.)

To appreciate the full irony of this situation with the fake priest, you have to bear in mind the dramatic stanzas of the well-known ballad 'The Croppy Boy', in which a yeoman captain fiendishly dons the soutane of a murdered priest to deceive and trap an unwary rebel. It's a characteristic linkage. Part of Kiely's unique gift is to register oblique connections and to draw what he needs from other people's experiences and other bodies of work to add richness and density to his own. It's a kind of productive rifling which is the opposite of plagiarism.

It has also to do with his irrepressible propensity for quotation and recitation: he simply can't help importing into his own narrative lines and verses from here, there and everywhere, most of which add to the gaiety and ebullience of his writing. A '"great man for the poetry"', says one of his characters about another in 'Bloodless Byrne of a Monday'. '"He could recite all night."' Indeed, the capacity for copious quotation seems to have been a family trait. In *Drink to the Bird*, his memoir of 1991, Kiely mentions his sister's ability to reel off pages from Walter Scott. And finally, in the book he published in 1996, *And as I Rode by Granard Moat*, he comes out in the open about his insatiable appetite for rhyme and recitation by putting together a collection of Irish songs and verses, all of which have been running through his head for years and years. Here, they are interspersed with a sparkling and idiosyncratic commentary: Kiely at his most fluent and voluble. The contents of this book include everything from James Clarence Mangan to 'The Boys of Mullaghbawn', from 'The Boyne Walk' to 'The Old Road Home'. You have 'The Woman of the Three Cows' alongside 'Nell

Flaherty's Drake'. You have Yeats and Francis Ledwidge and Cathal Buidhe Mac Giolla Gunna and 'The Man from God-Knows-Where'. But eclectic and wide-ranging as it is, *Granard Moat* represents only a fraction of the songs and poems Kiely had by heart, and which would keep bursting out of him at any moment, expected or unexpected.

When, for example, you read the opening lines of the strange story 'Eton Crop', which goes as follows:

> I had an uncle once, a man of three score years and three, and when my reason's dawn began he'd take me on his knee, and often talk, whole winter nights, things that seemed strange to me. He was a man of gloomy mood and few his converse sought ...

Reading this, you have to blink rapidly and look again: surely you must be seeing things. Are you drunk, or was the author, or the publisher, drunk? Who is this uncle of sixty-three, and what does he mean by keeping a young child up all night, ranting away at him in the manner of the Ancient Mariner? More to the point, what hideousness has overtaken Benedict Kiely's prose style? It's a relief to read on and find the author is merely quoting from an ancient book of dramatic recitations for children; he is, as ever, having fun with his faculty for committing to memory all manner of literary compositions and curiosities, and leading the reader up the garden path for the second or two it takes to reach the end of the atrabilious uncle.

It is tempting to regard Benedict Kiely as a short-story writer par excellence, and pay less attention to the rest of his prodigious output. But if his stories make the strongest impact, his novels aren't far behind, with their agreeably rambling structure and characteristically energetic approach. In fact, the novel came before the stories, starting in 1946 with *Land Without Stars*, which is set in County Tyrone and County Donegal. Other titles followed swiftly: *In a Harbour Green* (1949), *There was an Ancient House* (1955) and *The Captain with the Whiskers* (1960), among others. In *Dogs Enjoy the Morning* (1968), Kiely created an alter ego for himself, Peter Lane, who – like the author – is at one point a clerical student in hospital recovering from an old spinal injury, and about to renounce an already insecure vocation. The presence of so many attractive young nurses about his bed, Kiely used to joke, was the thing that brought him to his senses. The fictional Cosmona, where Peter Lane undergoes an identical experience, is at one level a quintessentially mad Irish village, and in it is enacted the age-old conflict between sex and celibacy, with the author coming down on the side of carnality and the carnivalesque – almost, it has to be said, to the point of saturation. We might find ourselves resorting to Philip Larkin's words: 'Too much confectionery, too rich'.

Kiely's first novel was preceded by a work of non-fiction, *Counties of Contention* (1945), which he described himself as 'a sort of romantic essay about the origins and implications of the partition of Ireland'. Having grown up in Omagh, which struck him as 'a pretty balanced and unbigoted town', and writing towards the end of the Second World War, with regeneration very much in the air, he believed a new spirit of tolerance and temperance in political and sectarian matters was about to overtake the Black North. He was encouraged in this opinion by something that happened during the writing of the book. Sitting in the National Library in Dublin, while engaged in research, Kiely became aware of a fellow-researcher sitting at the opposite side of his desk, and surrounded by piles of books very similar to those requested by Kiely himself. This was Hugh Shearman – a largely forgotten Belfast author – who was then working on one of his studies of Northern Ireland (possibly his *Anglo-Irish Relations* of 1948).

The two soon struck up a conversation. Kiely's brief was to show that partition was an anomaly based on disagreement and misunderstanding, and resulting in two fragments of a broken country; Shearman took the opposite line, arguing for the singularity of Ulster as a political and geographical entity whose ways had diverged from the rest of Ireland, going back to prehistoric times. Nevertheless, the two authors had a good deal in common, not least the wish to present their findings as impartially as possible. Soon they are exchanging views and recommendations, and drawing one another's attention to certain primary texts, which, if no use in furthering one of their purposes, might suit the thesis being propounded by the other. In this way, it happens that the mildly nationalist Kiely has considerable input into a defence of Unionism, while the mildly Unionist Shearman contributes equally to the anti-partitionist standpoint of Benedict Kiely. Here, it seems to me, we have a striking instance of the ironies and complexities inherent in any appraisal of 'Ulster'.

But Kiely's optimism about the future – his sense of 'new ideas, generous ideas' infiltrating the hidebound enclaves of the North – was not well-founded. He couldn't have predicted in the 1940s and 1950s the extent to which things in the future would fall apart: and it's in a very different frame of mind that he tackles, in his fiction, the irrepressible badness within the warring factions and its appalling outcome. The novella *Proxopera* (1977) and the novel *Nothing Happens in Carmincross* (1985) are bitter, angry works which capture the distortion of the old republican ideology as the terrorist atrocity bursts on the scene, with all its horrific power and effect. It's a terrible era in the history of the North, which shocks and bewilders erstwhile upholders of a principled opposition to perceived misgovernment. An old-style nationalism, whose erosion Kiely deplores, had nothing to do with blowing the legs off girls in coffee bars, or holding a man's family hostage while he drives a bomb to its target.

Proxopera and *Carmincross* are compelling exercises in indignation, but the tone of outrage does not come naturally to Benedict Kiely, whose primary impulse is to celebrate, to enshrine uproariously, to reminisce prolifically and pungently. He does all these in his vivid memoir *The Waves Behind Us*, with its abundant cast of characters, its folk-singers, literary editors, poets, performers of all kinds, men of letters, all 'civil and companionable men'. A Northerner by birth, a Dubliner by habitation, an excursionist for pleasure, Kiely, in his literary persona, identifies and unifies many aspects of Ireland and keeps his readers' spirits raised. Like that of William Carleton – of whom he wrote a fine biographical study – Kiely's writing is awash with energy and ingenuity. Also like Carleton, he keeps one foot, or at least one toe, in a darker reality.

When he ends his introduction to a reissue of Carleton's *Autobiography* (1996) with the words, 'He saw the little road lined with gallows. He saw the black horrors of famine. Around him in the ruin, and with him in his own soul were the makings of modern Ireland', you might apply the sentiment to Benedict Kiely himself, its particulars adapted to a twentieth-century reality.

JOHN WILSON FOSTER

•

The Light of Other Days: Revolving Many Memories

I. IN AND OUT OF TIME

Anniversaries can be occasions for grateful celebration which nonetheless chill and astonish at the passing of time when one's back, as it were, was turned. It's a hundred years since Benedict Kiely was born, and thus over half a century since I met him at the University of Oregon, both of us newly arrived in the far west, he as visiting creative writer in his mid-forties and under full sail. That it seems like yesterday is due in part to the unforgettable quality of the man, an acquainting of instant and lasting impact. The secure tenure of his memory for me contradicts his death and the loss of his friendship. This contradiction, as it happens, re-enacts in miniature what I believe to be the tension that inspired Kiely's life and work – between the irrecoverable nature of the past and the need, or wish, to imagine that past as the present, strained through time's sieve until the curious, marvellous and heroic remain, immune to time's passage. But the past becomes fully the present only after the painstaking retracings that are

Kiely's fictions – diversions and deferments being among the pains, unpleasurable and pleasurable alike.

As a doctoral student in English at the University of Oregon, I had to take courses and these involved a good deal of literary history, sequences of authors, works and genres. But most of the seminars were conducted along other lines, virtually under licence of the New Critics. In charge were two critical firms – they sounded and were treated like law firms: Wimsatt and Beardsley, Brooks and Warren. By day I was taught in the seminar rooms to disregard the author's intention (the intentional fallacy), indeed to disregard the author himself or herself as far as possible (the biographical fallacy), the impact of a literary work (the affective fallacy), and the social context in which the poem or novel had been written. We analysed intently the structure of the works, their architecture and image clusters, allowed only the latitude of identifying irony, itself a structural device. That way, the work was eternally in the present.

At night, in the taverns and restaurants of Eugene, it was very different. By my charismatic new mentor from Dublin and Omagh I was introduced by proxy into a previously unknown and clamorous world of writers' lives (mostly, but not exclusively, Irish) – all powered by song and quotation: life and literature piecemeal and wholesale. Ben knew or had met many writers of note, but those long dead whom he had never met were as though he *had* met them, as he quoted and resuscitated all of them, the living and the dead alike, until they sat beside us sharing our schooners and carafes.

This was neither literary history in the approved manner, nor undue respect for the integrity of self-contained works. This double abstention from academic literary history and close reading was practised in Kiely's published criticism, be it his 1947 critical life of William Carleton, his 1950 survey of post-Great War Irish fiction, or his miscellaneous essays and reviews collected in *A Raid into Dark Corners* (1999). And yet his promiscuous commerce with writers past and present had the curious effect of removing them from time and place as successfully as did the New Critics and was a form of reading completely aloof from fashionable concerns. Ben's ahistorical approach to literature was akin to E.M. Forster's in *Aspects of the Novel* (1927), whose readers were told that 'Time, all the way through, is to be our enemy'.[1] Like Forster, Ben imagined writers as contemporaneous members of a timeless company (his later role as Saoi of Aosdána was very fitting) and like Seamus Heaney – whom Ben discovered and encouraged early in his career – he retained a lifelong pleasure in belonging to the ancient guild of the pen. He subscribed, without attribution, to T.S. Eliot's notion of the presence of the past implicit in the latter's sense of tradition, which is not chiefly a matter of chronological succession but of the past living now, more palimpsest than chronology.[2] Which means that the present has as legitimate a claim on us as the past and when it came to song, for example, tradition in the popular sense was not essential.[3] Ben demonstrated the corollary of Eliot's idea of tradition. Despite our sense of his huge vocal personality, Ben's typical narrator, though controlling and very much a character, is mostly (save when recreating his own boyhood experiences) niggardly with information about himself, instead being in perpetual traffic with stories and characters, inside and outside literature. Ben's work was actually an escape from personality in Eliot's sense, his narrator preoccupied with remembering and incorporating the busy world beyond himself.[4]

Yet, despite this apparent obliviousness to chronology, Ben's sense of the relentlessness of life and passage of centuries was always there; he was aware of 'the pastness of the past', in Eliot's phrase. I remember his chuckling over Yeats's boast in 'The Tower' that the master had thought out Red Hanrahan's adversities 'twenty years ago', as if a score of years was more than a trice.[5] But he shared with Yeats a loyalty to friends and the acute sense of their loss. In his writings and conversation, Ben would recall absent or dead friends and dignify them in the manner of the poet of 'The Tower' or 'The Municipal Gallery Revisited', conscious, I assume, that memory can become commemoration and thus a victory of sorts against time's depredations. 'A Letter to Peachtree' ends with a series of vignettes separated by the 'stage direction': 'Time passes'. In one of those vignettes the (real-life) writer Brinsley MacNamara is quoted as saying that 'there is no time that is absolutely past' but also that there is 'little time in the present, it passes so quickly'. Friendship for Ben was foremost, as it was for the author of 'The Municipal Gallery Revisited', though it was unnecessary to be one of the Olympians to earn his friendship. He would have endorsed Thomas Moore's sad hymn to friendship in 'The Light of Other Days' and its lines 'Fond memory brings the light / Of other days around me', which is the motive-premise of most of Ben's stories. The central character of

'Bloodless Byrne of a Monday' blurrily recalls the first
of these lines in his hangover, as though memory can be
liberating.

II. TIMES PAST

Ben entitled his 1991 memoir *Drink to the Bird*, and
borrowed its epigraph from the desperate injunction in
Edwin Arlington Robinson's poem 'Mr. Flood's Party':[6]
'The bird is on the wing, the poets says, / And you and
I have said it here before. / Drink to the bird.' Old Eben
Flood is recalling 'The Rubaiyat of Omar Khayyam':
'The Bird of Time has but a little way / To fly – and Lo!
The Bird is on the Wing'. Ben was a formidable drinker;
but he always drank to the bird. Doing so was for Ben
a companionable, evocative, even creative response to
time passing; and it was of course a living metaphor as
well, for he wrote to the bird too, from dawn after dawn,
standing at his bureau like Hemingway, as if to pose a
defiance.

In Robinson's life was a drama of quiet desperation
that echoed a noisier, indeed declamatory, desperation
that Ben drew on in one of his best stories, 'Eton Crop'.
Young Robinson had been in love with Emma Shepherd,
but it was his older and more handsome brother, Herman,
who won her hand. Robinson took his loss badly and
thought bitterly that his brother had stolen Emma with
shallow charm. Herman died relatively young, after which
Robinson twice proposed to Emma. When she rejected
him, he left the town where he had hoped to live with her
and her three children, his three nieces.

'Eton Crop' is a story of intricate and, at the start, puzzling layering, not only of plotline but also of chronology – 1831, 1897, the 1930s and the 1980s, when the story appears to be narrated. Only at story's end would most readers know that the story begins with the Scottish lawyer-poet Henry Glassford Bell's 1831 Poe-like horror verse-tale, 'The Uncle. A Mystery'.[7] 'One night I do remember well', says the poem's adult narrator (which turns out to be laughable understatement). His uncle, having morosely contained his simmering guilt through the years, confesses to his barely understanding young orphan nephew that, vengefully jealous, he murdered his handsomer older brother, the boy's father, who had won the hand of the boy's mother, though his uncle had loved her first. Like Robinson, the uncle departs to forget, but cannot, and seeing, on his return, the doting husband and wife, decides to kill his brother. (Robinson's brother died prematurely with what must have seemed at first like a convenience that pre-empted the poet's darker thoughts.) On the night the adult nephew remembers so well, the fratricide opens a locked chest to show his young nephew the 'bare-ribbed skeleton' that had never been discovered. He is seized by the throat by what he believes to be his brother's ghost, falls back in a frenzy and dies. Out of possessive love, loss and murder, Bell attempted in his own absurdly melodramatic way to make art.

The entirety of 'The Uncle', a poem of twenty-four six-line stanzas, is woven by instalments into the narrative of 'Eton Crop', but as prose, thereby muffling the effect of quotation, confusing a first reading of the story. Towards the story's end, the narrator quotes his own love poem about Maruna, the girl with whom as a boy he was infatuated, but likewise not in verse: 'It looks better in prose as most poems would nowadays.' The narrator's recitation of Bell's 'woeful' poem is, we infer, from a book he was given two days before he is writing. It is a posthumous gift from Maruna via her son after her death the year before. The book is *Illustrated Recitations by R.C. Buchanan. The Uncle: Illustrated by Thirty-Six Photographical Reproductions.*[8] Kiely's narrator sardonically describes the accompanying photographs of Buchanan's evening-suited, melodramatic recitative postures after each few lines or stanzas. ('Eton Crop' is, among other things, a humorous eulogy to the vanished pre-television age of amateur and professional recitation and singing at home, at school, and on the concert stage.)[9]

Maruna had used the book in order to improve her concert recitations. She is nineteen and the narrator seventeen at the time the latter is recalling, her memory evoked by her posthumous keepsake gift. That was 'away before 1939' and one is tempted to place the story's central scene in 1936, when Kiely himself was seventeen. (Often in a Kiely story the gap between the narrator and the author seems narrow; in several stories, the parents of the narrator are called Tommy and Sara and the narrator called Ben; Kiely's father and mother were Tom and Sarah.) The narrator brings to mind a concert in the town hall in which he, in a state of nerves, is, with accompanying gestures, to recite Patrick Pearse's 'The Wayfarer' ('The beauty of the world hath made me sad, / This beauty that will pass') which Kiely prosifies in the narrator's recall. To recite this poem at the time was to glorify the Irish 'glorious dead' of Easter 1916, thus with beauty, violence and death commingling.

The young reciter disbelieves what he recites until the poem sadly hymns the children playing on the streets of little towns in Connacht, at which the reciter's surge of patriotism makes his performance convincing to his elder brother in the audience. In the wings, Maruna kisses him to dispel his stage fright before he goes on after her. She has just recited Elizabeth Barrett Browning's 'A Musical Instrument', with its opening gift for the reciter: 'What was he doing, the great god Pan / Down in the reeds by the river?' What he was doing was, in revenge, mutilating the reed into which her sisters had turned the nymph Syrinx to rescue her from the goat-hoofed god's pursuit, and making of it the pipe that then plays a music that calms and sweetens the nature he has violently disturbed in the making of the pipe: beauty, art and brutality again commingled.

Besides the narrator and Maruna, 'Eton Crop' has two other young couples, Eugene and Anna, and Belinda and the boxer, who sings familiar Irish songs on the stages of Irish towns. What connects the suite of couples is the Eton Crop hairstyle of the girls and the eventual failure of all the couplings: the story is one of loss and lost opportunity, some of it of course endemic to youth. The tacit difference between the worldly glamour of the Eton Crop and Hollywood movies and the tardy reality of small-town Irish life is another dimension of life's irony.[10] But Eugene's fate returns us to the ancillary theme of darkness and war. The ardour required to cycle ten miles up a mountain to see his inamorata faltered and he enlisted in 1939 and fought in an unspecified 'bloody battle that shook the world' and perhaps never came back.

The core action of 'Eton Crop' dates from the easy world the narrator knew between the Irish Troubles and the Second World War, when 'No warning bugles were blown'. Even so, it is a story of the merciless passage of time when opportunity is unseized. 'Should I have simply kissed back?' The narrator had felt Maruna's silken thigh in the cinema, but that was all. Thinking of 'I Told Every Little Star' ('Friends ask me am I in love / I always answer yes') the narrator concludes: 'a haunting song may return but a lost beauty never'.

Time and again in the stories, remembrance is of lost or unfulfilled love and of beauty now gone, with war playing a fitful role in all these. After Father Paul's death in 'A Great God's Angel Standing', Paul's friend, the rural rake Pascal Stakelum, discloses that Paul had on the eve of his death given him a book ('keep as a memory of me when I'm gone') he had once received from a young American woman when he was in Virginia, with a loving dedication in memory of 'a day of sunshine never to be forgotten' – beauty, we assume, lost to Father Paul owing to a reluctance or inability to grasp it. For his part, Pascal foresees, instead of remembering, the fate of beauty (Pearse's 'beauty that will pass', beauty lost not just to the beautiful but also to its beholders) when he is on a visit with Father Paul to the lunatic asylum and sees in elderly women that 'beauty was vain': 'This, in the ward before him, was what could happen to beauty.'

'Eton Crop' on an idle read might seem to be gabby and digressive, but it is in fact expertly controlled and with an inspired structure, as is 'A Great God's Angel Standing'. The latter, likewise, demonstrates the potent interaction of life and literature that is a hallmark of Benedict Kiely's art; past literature illuminates the present, and present experience reinterprets that past literature. Father Paul's gifted keepsake, bequeathed to Pascal, was an exquisite – possibly a Kelmscott Press – copy of William Morris's *The Defence of Guenevere and Other Poems* (from which Kiely took his story's title: Guenevere's image of the angel standing at the foot of the bed with the blue cloth of hell and the red cloth of heaven on offer). Pascal reads portions to the narrator, crudely but sympathetically, seeing parallels between the beautiful Guenevere and both Father Paul's admirer (assumed to be beautiful and wanting Paul) and the nurse from the asylum he himself once seduced.

The poem recounts what (luckily in this case) did *not* happen, but in the tragic story of Guenevere and Launcelot love and beauty are eventually lost. Here once again are art, beauty and the memory of pain and loss or missed opportunity. For characters, narrators and author alike, life and literature interpenetrate. In *Nothing Happens in Carmincross* (1985), a character argues 'that every experience is a quotation, and that every quotation is a renewed experience, a light switched on again in a darkened room to reveal familiar objects'. Literature for Ben was a bottomless fund of timeless wisdom and exemplary cases in human affairs. He made literature work its passage in life, throwing comparative light on the present and being ceaselessly relevant – more important, perhaps, than the incidental relish of a work's, or a writer's, uniqueness. Nothing new under the sun means all is new simultaneously. 'A Great God's Angel Standing' ends with the narrator imagining the poetry-loving Father Paul's last vision, sitting upright before he lowers his head to the table to die, his vision incorporating images from literature read and life lived (or too often, tragically not lived), the white flame of Guenevere, the white dogwood blossoms of Virginia: 'Looking straight ahead to Fincastle, Virginia, and seeing a woman white with flame when the dogwood blossomed, seeing the tall angel whose wings were the rainbow and who held heaven, a red cloth, in one hand, and hell, a blue cloth, in the other.'

The calling up in memory of changes through time and how they reduce life's possibilities and thwart fulfilment, despite the memorable compensations of the curious and beautiful, drives many of Ben's stories. As in 'Eton Crop', there is the memory of a girl unkissed by the narrator in 'The Little Wrens and Robins'. But even had she been kissed there was no guarantee of happiness. It is a heartbreaking gem of a story whose lesson is that whereas friendship can endure, love rarely does. And anticipating 'Eton Crop', there is poetry woven throughout; once again it is bad poetry (a hopeful hymn to spring), though this time written presumably by Kiely himself, as though by the narrator's cousin Ellen, who writes for the local newspapers' Poet's Corners. She marries a man and hopes for happiness because she believes 'love is all', but is abandoned by her husband and dies young, having nursed an undeclared love for a handsome priest.

The narrator quotes his cousin to reveal partly the extent of her delusion about her poetic powers and partly the pathos of the soon-to-be-unfounded optimism of her hymn to spring. But wisdom and truth work through popular and even bad art too, and the lives of the literary and unliterary alike share reversals. He is escorting through town, to her date with a 'fella', the Mayo girl who is his aunt's domestic, who is always singing but whose career on stage would be foiled by the discolouring birthmark on one cheek that would require her, cousin Ellen had said, to sing always with one side of her face away from the audience. When he tries to kiss her, she turns her face away and the story ends with his wondering what song she sings for her fella and (the Kiely touch) which side of her face she turns towards him. Before he tried to kiss her, she was singing, 'Ah, sweet mystery of life at last I've found you', a song from the operetta *Naughty Marietta* (1910, and a hit film in 1935) which is absolutely sure that 'it is love alone that rules for aye' – the secret of the mystery of life.

But 'The Little Wrens and Robins' poignantly illustrates that solving the mystery does not mean love is for aye. As the central character of 'Bloodless Byrne of a Monday' muses, 'the old order changeth yielding place to new'. He is unobtrusively quoting Tennyson's dying King Arthur from the 'dusky barge' in which he has been placed. With Kiely facility, the barge becomes one of Dublin's vanished brewery barges and King Arthur becomes Arthur Guinness of equally immortal memory because the Tennyson line was once a caption to a cartoon of top-hatted Arthur Guinness standing among the stout barrels when lorries were about to supersede barges.[11]

Kiely's risk-taking with sentimentality and popular art is one of his characteristics. The incidental richness of detail in his stories (using a map, we can track the narrator and his cousin Ellen through the streets of Omagh town, unnamed in the story), the constant lateral observations, the occasional sardonicism of the narrator, the impression of a narratorial mind fully alert – these ensure that the sentimentality is strategic, something he shares with the author of *Dubliners*.

III. REWINDING TIME

Watching the barge carry Arthur away, Sir Bedivere stands 'revolving many memories'. Ben Kiely's narrators do likewise, and time is often rotated and rewound as his characters embark on journeys back to recover the heroic past and its distant source, often through layers of years and generations (and, notably, wars). The journeyer can be an Irish expatriate (typically returned from America), Irish descendant or native. The journeys, by the writer's use of landscape and symbolism, effortlessly assume archetypal significance in the manner of folktales of the quest variety while retaining the necessary realism of the short story.

In 'Homes on the Mountain', the narrator recalls (perhaps in the 1960s) being taken at twelve years of age with his brother (perhaps in the early 1930s) by their father in search of two relatives across dark hills that the father walked as a youth (perhaps in the 1880s). They find the unmarried elderly brothers but also dilapidation, barrenness, shadows of former allegedly passionate selves, and paradise (which must now subsist only in the memory) ruined by time and modernity. In 'A Journey to the Seven Streams', the father again leads the family, this time in a broken-down car in search of a stone fiddle, elusive relic of a vanished eighteenth-century baronial past of minstrelsy and revelry. This comic mock-epic quest fails to find the fiddle and the questers satisfy themselves with picnicking 'in a meadow by the cross-roads in the exact centre of the wide saucer of land where seven streams from the surrounding hills came down to meet. The grass was polished with sunshine. The perfume of the meadowsweet is with me still.' 'The peace of heaven is here', says the mother when her husband expresses disappointment at not reaching their original destination. Paradise regained and the timeless source of life are but briefly apprehended. When the narrator relives the journey years later as his father's body is returned from Donegal, the meadowland saucer has seemed to shrink and fiddle music has been silenced by television.

In 'The Heroes in the Dark House', an elderly and local amateur folklorist collects Irish hero tales told him by fireside storytellers 'for whom there was only the past'. The tellers do not only tell tales of quests to the ends of the earth but also travel with the heroes in their imaginations as they talk. The present becomes the past. The collector himself is receding into the past, beaten to publication of his collected tales by a young scholar from a neighbouring town. He recalls lost friendships, including that with Thomas Andrews who built the *Titanic*; he also thinks of the folktale characters as real, fusing past and present. The story's structure is appropriately circular, the second of its six sections being a flashback and the first section continuing the conversation of the sixth. It is set in 1944 when American troops in Northern Ireland in the village above the garrison town (Omagh but unnamed) are mustering on the eve of D-Day. A major had commissioned the collector to assemble his tales for distribution to the troops. But the next morning the troops have gone and it doesn't happen.

In the first section the collector hosts the young scholar he had invited to his house and tells him the story he introduced in the last section – the overnight vanishing of the troops. But already the American troops have joined the British soldiers of 1798 (hostile, unlike the Americans) in his ageing imagination, along with the pikemen who fought them and the heroes of the ancient tales. All the heroes are, at the same time, in his own dark house, grey shadows enveloped by the smoke from his fire. They are, of course, his friends, as the tales were his children. In the collector's clouded mind, all have become images like those from the Great Memory of Yeats's 'The Tower' – that imperishable storehouse of the memorable. They live as genuinely for the collector as they did for Yeats, whose bedroom still hosted the medieval ghosts at dice. In his Yeats-like 'fantastical imagination', the collector is his creator's understudy. But Kiely, like the poet, is also clearheaded and composed in his fictional vision of Time's defeat and the halting of the Bird in flight.

PAUL CLEMENTS

•

The Traveller

From September 1964 until the summer of 1968, Benedict Kiely spent terms as writer-in-residence in several different parts of the USA. In 1964, at the age of forty-five, he was first of all based at Hollins College, Virginia. The following year he served as visiting professor in creative writing at the University of Oregon in Eugene. And in 1966 he was appointed writer-in-residence at Emory University, Atlanta, Georgia, returning to Ireland in 1968.

America was pure gold for Ben. It presented an opportunity to travel around various states, explore the country, drink in new landscapes and cityscapes, meet the people and develop his students' writing skills. From New England through the mid-west and Deep South and across to the west coast, he travelled, lectured and taught widely, perceptively capturing the many faces of the United States.

Ben was especially active for *The Irish Times*, contributing a regular 'Letter from America', which appeared fortnightly. Each letter was a substantial production, running to some 2,500 words. Travel writing is an open-ended genre, with wide parameters and enormous elasticity, and America comes alive in these letters. Everywhere he went he kept notebooks and scraps of paper as aides-mémoire and was constantly alert to the numerous anecdotes and *obiter dicta* that enliven his dispatches.

Even though 3,000 miles and an ocean separated him from Ireland, it often played a part in his writing and became a leitmotif in the letters. In one, he refers to growing up in Omagh, and to its rivers and lakes, which meant so much to him. He charted life in different states, analysed the culture, and marvelled at the California redwoods. He memorably portrays arriving in Chicago, where the landscape changes from a dead cornland to an industrial city:

> Here's an overhead freeway and a shanty town below: a clover-leaf with demented, spinning traffic: puffs of industrial smoke, white, brown, black and grey, increasing in number until it would seem as if the earth was erupting; and a million railtracks and a million parallel rows of housing: and Lake Calumet Harbour and a prospect of desolation, brown marsh, brick rubble, three tall red-and-white chimneys, a huge billboard from which a moustachioed old-timer offers you the gasoline that won the west.

He connects the scene to an *Irish Times* colleague, Mary Maher, who was born in Chicago, and ends the piece with an impish, self-deprecating comment: 'But far ahead there are soaring buildings and a flying suspension bridge that glistens, and over there is Chicago and the lake: Mary Maher Country, where it behooves a spalpeen like myself to walk with respect' ('On the Road to Chicago and the Great Lakes', *The Irish Times*, 20 April 1967).

Ben adopted a travel reportage style, recording his impressions, ferreting out titbits of information on the American melting pot and filling his features with the unpredictability of human nature. His sojourn gave him the opportunity to write about subjects as diverse as Basque shepherds who squirted wine from a goatskin pouch in Oregon, the Mormon buildings of Salt Lake City, or time spent in Atlanta wandering among the skyscrapers: 'Atlanta is not so much an ordinary city as a shapeless giant of a suburb that began to grow, as if when asleep, in a forest whose limbs sprawl here and there and everywhere in the shade of timber' ('Early Morning U.S.A.', *The Irish Times*, 8 December 1966). The enthusiasm and eccentricities of Americans appealed to him. Ben loved the quirky side of Californian life, where he discovered in San Francisco a J.M. Synge play being performed in Chinatown, while at the Playhouse on Fisherman's Wharf he was delighted to see posters for Brendan Behan's *The Hostage*. In Georgia, he listened to a young fundamentalist preacher named Ian Paisley speaking at a Baptist tabernacle, and admired the gigantic Mr Peanut sign, a popular American advertising symbol and mascot of the Planters snack-food company.

Looking through the faded newspaper clippings and handwritten holographs produces a frisson, illustrating the elegance of Ben's expression and whisking the reader back fifty-five years. Greyhound buses or trains were his favourite mode of travel and often led to serendipitous encounters and chance remarks which would later appear in his work. Public transport, he wrote, was 'cheap, efficient and comfortable, and the best place to casually meet the plain people of America'. Entire days were spent on a Greyhound bus when '27 hours of travail' brought him from Des Moines, Iowa, by way of Nebraska and Wyoming into the state of Utah. He enjoyed the trains, too, especially the long transcontinental service known as the Domeliner which had several carriages with a second storey capped by a glass dome and was somewhere to sit like a king watching the world swim by:

> Two freight trains placed end to end would equal the entire CIÉ empire. This dome I sit in is a fit tower for a poet and I would like to see Patrick Kavanagh here because I know that his high and simple mind would appreciate the wonder of it. It would also keep him from destroying his poems by growling about the neighbours, the dacent townies from the County Tyrone ('Train through Oregon', *The Irish Times*, 9 June 1966).

The personable and informal style of Ben's writing was ideal for a newspaper readership. It also made his travels around Ireland companionable, forming an important part of his non-fiction and often returning to overarching themes: Catholic faith, Irish nationalism, literary criticism and the landscape. He had the ability to weave a huge amount of detail into his high-spirited stories, including countryside description, the etymology of place-names, legends and fables, snippets of poems, songs and curiosity. His precise way with words, and above all his inclusive sense of historical knowledge, makes his travel writing, and in particular his major travel narrative on Ireland, *All the Way to Bantry Bay and other Irish Journeys*, stand apart. Consider this sentence inspired by the area around Dromore, County Tyrone, where he was born: 'The jostling mixum-gatherum of Irish history is all around us, but what country isn't in a similar state and, God above, think of what America has gatherumed and mixumed in a short two centuries.'

All the Way to Bantry Bay includes the author's digressive wanderings through Tyrone, Fermanagh, Antrim, Donegal, Monaghan, Galway, Laois, Offaly, Tipperary and Cork. Some of the journeys for his research were made in the spring of 1969, so the book had a long gestation. Fifty years on, it has become an eloquent period piece of topographical and literary writing and a valuable social document. Ben was always alive to the textures of Irish life and his book is filled with vivid on-the-road reminiscences and vignettes of places he frequently visited, along with engaging stories providing colour and richness. It shows his ability to evoke the spirit of place – the *genius loci* – often apparent in just a few words: Errigal in Donegal is 'the Cock o' the North, silvery, clear-cut'; in west Cork, he refers to the remote Coomhola area as 'the valley of a million sheep'. With his love of literature, he frequently invokes other writers and has many literary enthusiasms. Almost unnoticed, he slips in a quote from Shakespeare, a mention of Edward Thomas, George Borrow and William Thackeray's *The Irish Sketchbook* (1842), which he regarded as one of the best books on Ireland ever written by an Englishman.

It is a pleasure to dip into *All the Way to Bantry Bay*, not just for information, but also for the warmth of Ben's style and the breadth of his knowledge which he generously shares with readers. He was shaped by the power of certain books. In Sligo, he said that he had finished reading, writing and broadcasting about Máire MacNeill's classic work *The Festival of Lughnasa*: 'My imagination, such as it was and is, had been much affected by her account of those places, on hilltops or by lakeshores where for centuries our ancestors had met to rejoice over the first fruits of harvest and to honour the god Lugh.' Ben's was a life saturated with mythology, local lore and folk sayings. His travel book contains snatches of half-forgotten songs, quotations recalled from old street ballads and odd fragments of verse, while elsewhere he draws on the work of archaeologists and antiquarians. His ability to sum up the essence of a landscape succinctly is noted in an afterword written by Thomas Kilroy to the novel *The Captain with the Whiskers*, republished in 2004: 'He has a detailed knowledge of landscape and all the associations of a particular place. This sense of place permeates his work, what he himself once called "the interweaving of love and imagination and locality".'

His native Tyrone – and its writers – were always uppermost. Although he left the county to settle in Dublin, he remained under its spell, frequently tapping into his well of memory for inspiration from childhood. He carried a map of the county in his mind, with its lyrical townland names firmly imprinted on it, as he explained in a personal section of the Tyrone chapter of *32 Counties: Photographs of Ireland* ... (1989):

If I were sending to Tyrone a friend who had never been there before, I would naturally send him first to my home town, Omagh, and to my friends therein, and after that, by Gortin and Plumbridge, Crannagh, into the Sperrins, along the Glenelly River, under the shadows of Sawel and Dart mountains to look in our legendary Glanconkyne ... Then, on to emerge by Slieve Gallen Braes, renowned in a famous ballad, at Cookstown and on to the lough shore at the High Cross of Ardboe.

In this topographical incantation, Ben does not mention the Clogher Valley in south Tyrone, a place to which he was strongly attached and which was the homeland of William Carleton. In the preface to *A Raid into Dark Corners and Other Essays* – published to mark Ben's eightieth birthday – John Montague, then Ireland Professor of Poetry, wrote that it was not Graham Greene or James Joyce who was his true literary godfather, but Carleton.

Over the years, Ben was a regular visitor to the ancient hill of Knockmany, the 'hill of Queen Baine', or *cnoc mBaine*, rising abruptly three kilometres north of Augher, not far from the border with County Monaghan. Draw one straight line westwards from Belfast and another straight line eastwards from Ballyshannon, County Donegal, and their intersection will be on the summit of Knockmany. The hill reaches a lowly 235 metres but dominates the landscape, providing a wide panorama; it was a place where Ben loved spending time. A round cairn on a clearing on the summit crowns the remains of the North's most decorative passage-tomb, dating from around 3000–2500

B.C. The upright stones of the chamber are ornamented with megalithic art similar to that found on the passage-tombs on the Loughcrew hills of County Meath.

Carleton, the son of a small tenant farmer, was born in 1794 in a whitewashed cottage at Prillisk, near Clogher, and one of his stories was 'The Legend of Knockmany'. Ben's biography of Carleton, *Poor Scholar* (1947), opens with a lyrical, cinematic and precise description that captures the fertile south Tyrone countryside of drumlins and villages:

> It is not mountainy land. It is not flat land. The tarred roads, linking the little towns together, rise and fall regularly over round rich hills, farmed to the top, held in place by a network of deep whispering hedges. Here and there the primitive force of the earth revolts from rich greenery, from fruitful furrows drawn by the rigid coulter; rises up into sombre moorland, or a ridge covered with coarse heather, or a hill planted with straight trees. The roads rise and fall, dropping into little glens where the leaves and the roadside grasses are unbelievably quiet, going over round hills to open up vistas of infinite blue distances, with mountains very low and far away on an uncertain horizon.

One of the numerous aspects of his busy life was radio broadcasting. Many listened to what John Montague called the 'rich, reverberating tones of his great organ voice' on the popular RTÉ Radio 1 programme *Sunday Miscellany*, which helped make Ben Kiely a household name. The oral tradition is important in his work. There is physicality in his stories and the melody of song rises in his rivers, valley and mountain descriptions with short declarative sentences. Often he introduces colloquialisms, snippets of rhyme, recitations, doggerel, and ballads by writers such as the Reverend W.F. Marshall, who came from Sixmilecross and was known as 'The Bard of Tyrone'. Ben said it was an honour to know him and to be able to recite one of his best-known poems of comic dialect, 'Me an' Me Da'.

Scores of magazines and literary journals as diverse as *The New Yorker* and *Ireland of the Welcomes* published his short stories and travel articles made up of the famed Ben mix of history, nostalgia and reflection. With his scrupulous eye for tiny details, his lightness of touch and high fun-quotient, he takes the reader with him, whether it is 'A Journey to the Seven Streams' or 'A Letter to Peachtree.' There is a line from a character which he quotes in *Nothing Happens in Carmincross*, 'Every experience is a quotation'. For Ben, everything appeared to trigger anecdotes and release a tumble of stories or aspect of language, and he had a pitch-perfect ear for dialogue. In *A Raid into Dark Corners*, he writes that in the southern American states, where many people with Ulster vowel sounds settled, he had come across a county in Alabama where some people had, by and large, a Tyrone accent.

Writers such as Colum McCann have absorbed Ben's perceptions and owe him a debt of gratitude, while he in turn was inspired by numerous novelists and poets. In *A Raid into Dark Corners*, John Montague states that: 'He is also unabashed in his nostalgia, his love of places and people who love them … he prefers his palimpsest of paraphrase and praise, to point us to the pleasures of the works he loves: Ben-evolence is his best critical method.'

In addition to his main travel book on Ireland, Ben dipped his pen into several large-format volumes of travel-related literature which bear his name on the cover as compiler, anthologist or contributor, showing the breadth of his inquisitive mind. *The Aerofilms Book of Ireland from the Air* (1985) presents a panoramic view of all four provinces, for which Ben wrote the text. Stunning aerial pictures complement his enthusiasm for the built heritage, mountains, lakes and rivers, and the unique landscape of places such as the Burren in Clare and the Curragh of Kildare. Another lavishly illustrated book celebrating the spirit of the country is *Yeats's Ireland: An Illustrated Anthology* (1989), to which Ben contributes a 5,000-word essay on the poet. A personal ramble around all four provinces through the eyes of writers, singers, poets and travellers is captured in his collection *And as I Rode by Granard Moat* (1996). Ben's wide-ranging anthology highlights such poems as Thomas MacDonagh's translation from the Irish of Cathal Buidhe Mac Giolla Gunna's 'The Yellow Bittern', Padraic Colum's 'The Old Woman of the Roads', the singer Delia Murphy with 'The Lambs on the Green Hills', and J.J. Callanan's 'Gougaune Barra'.

Dublin was where Ben lived for most of his adult life and he published two books about the city. In 1983, he compiled, with an introduction, a slim volume in the Small Oxford Books series, simply called *Dublin*. A city long celebrated in novels, plays and poems called for, he realised, such an anthology, especially from an outsider

– an Ulsterman. The pocket book takes the form of a bus journey around the suburbs and into the city centre. It covers history, politics and literature, with accounts of the passing of the Act of Union as witnessed by Thomas De Quincey and of the funeral of Ireland's 'Uncrowned King', Charles Stewart Parnell. He explores the Coombe and the Liffey with the comedian Jimmy O'Dea and his friend Harry O'Donovan, giving life to the legendary street trader 'Biddy Mulligan the Pride of the Coombe'. Entering into the picture with the Dublin comedians is 'Mrs Maxwell' from Belfast's Sandy Row, the parodic creation of Richard Hayward, one of the most prolific travel writers from the middle decades of the twentieth century. The author of eleven topographical studies of different regions of Ireland, Hayward was also a renowned actor and singer, and well-known to Ben, who refers in his Dublin anthology to Hayward's 'excellent' travel books. He came across them through his reviewing with *The Irish Times*, using the pen name 'Patrick Lagan', which he shared with Seán White.

His second book on the capital, *25 Views of Dublin* (1994), centres on an exhibition of prints by the architect James Horan. Based on James Mahon's original series of drawings between 1792 and 1799, Horan produced a corresponding set of twenty-five views. Ben wrote the commentary on each of the streets or buildings, including Trinity College, the Rotunda in Parnell Street, Dublin Castle, St. Patrick's Cathedral, the Casino at Marino, and a particular favourite, Westland Row, where he often walked with Brinsley MacNamara, author of, among other works, *The Valley of the Squinting Windows*:

When I had the honour and privilege of becoming a friend of Brinsley MacNamara, that promenade acquired an added significance. Brinsley liked to walk in stately fashion in the Row. He was then secretary of the National Gallery, where I would call for him. Then an inspection of the books in Greene's. Then round two corners and into the Row. Down all the way and up again. A brief pause in Kennedy's for a sip and a bit of philosophy. Then round another corner and via Lincoln Place to take the air on the green ground of Trinity College. To salute Lecky, the great historian, and to emerge between Goldsmith and Burke. And Brinsley talking of Delvin and the midlands and his memories. No brains could have brought me on a more instructive journey.

Equally instructive is Ben's own travel writing, whether around Ireland or in America, overflowing with musicality, erudition and wit. It illustrates the intensity of a watchful writer who could illuminate places with memorable images, creating a window on a new world, as well as on a vanishing one. Penned by the hand of a maestro, his travel writing shows that he was a repository of stories, a raconteur and *seanchaí* par excellence, with a remarkable knowledge of history coupled with a passion and zest for life.

CHRISTOPHER CAHILL

•

'I Was the Stranger Who Had Once Been the Guide': Benedict Kiely's Americans

'It's a long way to Buffalo,' as the song says. 'It's a long way to Belfast City too.' Omagh, County Tyrone – Benedict Kiely's home town, wellspring, *omphalos* and land of heart's desire – seems in his stories, novels and memoirs so much a place apart that it might, in its peace, lie equidistant from both those cities, other than when the chaotic realities of each manage to threaten and disrupt the work, ease and order of the town and its countryside around. Affection for the home place saturates Kiely's work. In 'A Journey to the Seven Streams' the narrator says:

> My father, the heavens be his bed, was a terrible man for telling you about the places he had been and for bringing you there if he could and displaying them to you with a mild gentle air of proprietorship ... [T] ownlands like Corraheskin, Drumlish, Cornavara ... and small towns like Drumquin and Dromore were all within a ten-mile radius of our town and something of

moment or something amusing had happened in every one of them.

The enunciation of the place names serves as a kind of litany, a telling of devotion to the hearth and the land, the ancestors, relations and community.

Which is not to say that Omagh is presented in Kiely's work as a kind of Brigadoon. It was a garrison town of the British Army during Kiely's youth, and, bright as it is, it is always inflected by a harsher worldliness, often presented as exterior or imported, but undeniably present regardless. One of the threads in Kiely's story 'Down then by Derry' (one of his great accomplishments as a fiction writer) involves the recollection and revisitation of a teenage hesitancy before the threshold of sexual experience. This awkward adolescent stumbling forward and away is counterpointed by the coarse, efficient trade of two local whores, uncharitably dubbed the Jennet and the Bluebottle:

> The Bluebottle vanished ahead of them into some riverside bushes. Where the river made an elbow bend a group of smoking muttering men waited at the Jennet's corner. Her shady bower was a wooden shelter put there by the town council to protect Sunday walkers from sudden showers. The council had not intended to cater for the comfort of the Jennet and her customers. She was a raw-boned red-headed country girl whose husband was in the mental hospital.

But the defining nature of the place is warm, rooted, continuous. It is home. For the third of the three epigraphs in the opening section of his last and darkest novel, *Nothing Happens in Carmincross*, Kiely gives the following from Eamon de Valera's 1943 St. Patrick's Day radio broadcast to the Irish people and characterises it as 'An [*sic*] euphoric or idiotic statement by a well-known twentieth-century Irishman of Spanish and Irish origins':

> The Ireland which we have dreamed of would be the home of a people who valued material wealth only as a basis of right living, of a people who were satisfied with frugal comfort and devoted their lives to things of the spirit; a land whose countryside would be bright with cosy homesteads, whose fields and villages would be joyous with sounds of industry, with the romping of sturdy children, the contests of athletic youths, the laughter of comely maidens; whose firesides would be forums for the wisdom of old age. It would, in a word, be the home of a people living the life that God desires men should live.[1]

Euphoric, perhaps, but thirty-five years further along with *der untergang des Abenlandes* it rings less idiotic, to one reader at least, and closer, indeed – if some shadows and regrets were to be added – to Kiely's Omagh than to the country of The Rubberbandits and Project Ireland 2040. Preferences may vary, but might we stop referring to it as progress?

Most of Kiely's writing life was lived away from Omagh, in Dublin, for the most part, in Rathgar and Donnybrook, with an annual pilgrimage home. The work at the desk, though, was punctuated by a considerable bit of roaming, almost all of which had a professional rationale or outcome. There is unlikely ever to have been another Irish writer who travelled Ireland so fully and deeply as Kiely did, in the 1950s and 1960s, when he was working as a newspaper man as well as producing many of his finest stories and novels. Thomas Flanagan, one of Kiely's closest American friends and literary peers, gives a fine description of this time and patter in his introduction to *The State of Ireland* (1980):

> When I first met Kiely and became friends with him, some twenty years ago, he was literary editor of the *Irish Press*, for which he also wrote an idiosyncratic column of travels around the country. I used often accompany him, and like other friends found it an exhilarating but disconcerting experience. A trip that ordinary clock time should have taken four or five hours at most would mysteriously stretch itself into days or even a week. At every twist in the road there would be a stream to watch or a crooked bridge to lean upon, and in every other village there would be someone to visit.

A portion of these writings, some of them first published under the pen-name Patrick Lagan, were collected as *All the Way to Bantry Bay and other Irish Journeys* (1978). In the title piece of that collection, Kiely declares that 'the purpose of this exercise or expedition is to get the four of us, the Californian, the Manhattan Islander, the red-bearded Limerick man and myself, as far as Dunboy that was once the fort of O'Sullivan Beare.'[2] The other three along with Kiely on this journey, easily identifiable in the literary and journalistic circles of the Ireland of the day, were, in the order presented, Thomas Flanagan, already author of *The Irish Novelists 1700–1850* (1959), later of *The Year of the French* (1979) and other novels, and at that time the Chair of the English Department at the University of California, Berkeley; Kevin Sullivan, author of *Joyce Among the Jesuits* (1958) and, prospectively but never conclusively, of an account of the forced march of O'Sullivan Beare following the defeat of the Irish at Kinsale in 1601; and David Hanly, writer and RTÉ broadcaster, and subsequently author of the novel *In Guilt and In Glory* (1979). This was one of those exhilarating and self-perpetuating journeys mentioned above, and while it is a challenge beyond the capacities of the present writer even to begin to summarise the narrative, nostalgic and recitative cross-currents Kiely adduces in his account of it – as he says himself, at the end of one tremendous run of associative dexterity, 'everything in Ireland reminds me of something else' – I wade into it because it was itself an echo of an earlier trip made by Kiely and Sullivan to the latter's ancestral home in Kerry.

This Kerry excursion would form the basis of Kiely's warmly eerie story (are there other works of literature that may be so described?), 'The Dogs in the Great Glen', to which I will return, and also allow Kiely himself to be heard in regard to the fits and starts of his circumambulations:

On the way back to Dublin from that wildest of all carnivals myself and a South African Jewish journalist who, for various good reasons, was not going back to South Africa, encountered here a poet and a friend of his who were down for the fishing. They leaned on the bridge under the shadow of the great castle and studied the water, and we joined them and stayed two jovial days in Cahir, and on the way back to Dublin lay in the sun on the grass on the top of Dunamase and heard the jackdaws screaming around the ruins of the castle that had changed hands so often in ancient wars; and steamed the last of the free champagne of Cork out of our clotted veins.

The poet, by the way, was Patrick MacDonagh and that was the same bridge that Flanagan mentions, though again on an earlier trip, a different one, that the four were then partially retracing.

Less familiar and never collected are Kiely's 'Letters from America', written for the *Irish Times* during his stateside university teaching sojourns in the mid-1960s. American wakes and returned Americans had been threaded through Kiely's writing before this period, and sometimes American soldiers stopping down in non-neutral Northern Ireland on their way to the great forced fratricidal war over in Europe. But there had been no direct notation of the States themselves. In certain respects, the 'Letters' make peculiar reading. Kiely's usual bonhomie, compassion, curiosity and fellow-feeling towards persons met in passing are present throughout. But one senses a failure – and an inner recognition of it – to manage a full embrace of the vast, mystifying, pointlessly threatening dystopian carnival that he is encountering:

The sage, really purple this evening, endless and lonely, is the whole world … The bus is loud with the laughter of young army men and their wives travelling all the way to Seattle … In Peyton, Idaho, the wandering labourers, young and old, slender-legged, in dungarees, look lonely and out of it all. Two young ones – they have no English – look long and longingly at the local, bare-legged female teenagers crowding the bright drug store, sipping coke and root beer.[3]

The relative rootlessness that many visitors to America have remarked upon registers especially strongly and particularly with the deeply rooted Kiely. The connectedness that is ever-present in his ramblings around Ireland, where everything reminds him of something else, is severed here and he finds himself facing into a blizzard of the random:

In Worcester, Mass., during a visit by Vice-President Hubert H. Humphrey, a time capsule has been buried to be dug up in five hundred years. It contains a mini-skirt, a Batman comic book, a Bible, Beatles records, a tape-recording made by John H. Glenn in orbit, a copy of John F. Kennedy's 1962 message to Congress, credit cards, an issue of *Playboy*, tranquilliser pills, etc. … If we're around in 2466, we may need those pills … My friend Manuelo, in the El Quijote on 23rd and 7th N.Y. says, 'It helps to be crazy and if you can't be crazy be drunk.'

These dispatches are also haunted by violence, motiveless and stupidly motivated: 'It is reported that a Bowery drifter, one of three "turned into human torches by teenagers" in one week, has died of burns. While sleeping in a doorway he was doused with kerosene and set aflame ... Arise, and bid me strike a match!' This American violence soon began to make its way into Kiely's fiction and seems somehow, if only through a kind of unliterary allusion, to be a source of or influence upon the violence soon to enflame Northern Ireland and centrally occupy Kiely's late writing, most notably in *Proxopera* and *Nothing Happens in Carmincross*.

'What happens to murderers who just never get caught?' Kiely asks in a 'Letter' written from a Howard Johnson motel in Atlanta. The newspaper story that prompted the reflection lingered with him and made its way into a scene in 'Down then by Derry', in which the narrator, home to Ireland and Omagh from America, falls into conversation at the hotel bar with some 'commercial men':

> —By God, they said, they have picturesque murders
> out there. We never have anything here except an
> odd friendly class of a murder. But out there ...
> —The one that sticks most in my mind ...

> They were all attention.

> —... was the girl in the sump. This sump is an
> overflow pond at the back of a dry-cleaning plant.
> One morning a man walking by sees a girl's leg
> standing up out of the water ...

—All for love, they said.

The long cold day, the search for the past, the drink, the warm company, had made him maudlin.

—When I read the newspapers today there are times I think I was reared in the Garden of Eden.

—Weren't we all, they said.

That garden, where things are, or at least once have been, as they should for the most part be, has for Kiely a precise and immovable location. America – one of the few places outside Ireland ever to feature substantially in Kiely's writing – is, in the end, immiscible.

—They're lining up to get into America, the son said.

—To get out of it too, son.

Returning tells a story of discovery every bit as revealing as the story of venturing forth, as 'Down then by Derry' details. And so also does 'The Dogs in the Great Glen', a story as fine as any Kiely or anyone else wrote at the time.[4] The first lines of the story give almost all there is of plot and dilemma, apart from the outcome:

The professor had come over from America to search out his origins and I met him in Dublin on the way to Kerry where his grandfather had come from and where he had relations, including a grand-uncle, still living.

'But the trouble is,' he said, 'that I've lost the address my mother gave me. She wrote to tell them I was coming to Europe. That's all they know. All I

121

remember is a name out of my dead father's memories:
the great Glen of Kanareen.'

The place is not to be found on any map, a not uncommon
phenomenon when place-names of folk memory emigrate
between both continents and languages.

'I have a middling knowledge of the Kerry mountains,'
I said. 'I could join you in the search …

'There are more things in Kerry than were ever
dreamt of by the Ordnance Survey. The place could
have another official name. At the back of my head I
feel that once in the town of Kenmare in Kerry I heard
a man mention the name of Kanareen.'

And so the professor and his Irish guide embark in search
of the glen, and they proceed, extemporaneously if not
arbitrarily, by way of the Knockmealdown mountains,
Mount Mellary, Coole Park and Galway City, until they
arrive in Kenmare, from where they are directed vaguely
eastwards.

At this point, an atmospheric and temporal shifting and
gradation begins that will swell and intensify throughout
the rest of the story.

The road twisted on across moorland that on our left
sloped dizzily to the sea, as if the solid ground might
easily slip and slide into the depths. Mountain shadows
melted like purple dust into a green bay. Across a
ravine set quite alone on a long, slanting, brown knife
blade of a mountain, was a white house with a red

door. The rattle of our pathetic little car affronted the vast stillness. We were free to moralise on the extent of all space in relation to the trivial area that limited our ordinary daily lives.

Everything quietens and slows down. Their local conductors, directing them towards a goal that seems ever more distant the closer they approach, take on an archaic aspect, silent watchers beyond the need of speech.

The two old druids of men resting from work on the leeward side of a turf-bank listened to our enquiry with the same attentive, half-conscious patience they gave to bird-cries or the sound of wind in the heather. Then they waved us ahead towards a narrow cleft in the distant wall of mountains as if they doubted the ability of ourselves and our conveyance to negotiate the Gap and find the Glen. They offered us strong tea and a drop out of a bottle. They watched us with kind irony as we drove away. Until the Gap swallowed us and the hazardous, twisting track absorbed all our attention we could look back and still see them, motionless, waiting with indifference for the landslide that would end it all.

There is nothing overtly mystical in the story and yet there is a saturating sense of transformation and transmigration, between the narrator and the professor, them both and the landscape; the Irishman lost for once in Ireland and the Irish-American coming ever closer to his ancestral home and identity; the present they share and the past of the professor's forebears and the stories of those people here, in this place, that had been present to him only as stories until this encounter with the soil known, it seems impossible to explain otherwise, to and by his blood.

'Of all my friends,' Thomas Flanagan once wrote of Kiely, 'he has, I think, the most copious and variously equipped memory – stored with Balzac, Chekhov, Shelley, Carl Jung, Hilaire Belloc, Plato, the verses of obscure or anonymous bards. All, great or small, are given a democratic welcome, as though his memory were a public house into which they have strolled for a drink or a chat.'

There is a beautiful juncture in 'The Dogs in the Great Glen' just before the travellers abandon the car and set off on shank's mare for the last ascent of the Gap, and I am going to suggest that at this point the shades of Hugo von Hofmannsthal and his Lord Chandos are also not out of place in that well-populated public house to which Flanagan refers.

By a roadside pool where water-beetles lived their vicious secretive lives, we sat and rested, with the pass and the cliffs, overhung with heather, behind us and another ridge ahead. Brazenly the sheer rocks reflected the sun and semaphored at us. Below us, in the dry summer, the bed of a stream held only a trickle of water twisting painfully around piles of round black stones. Touch a beetle with a stalk of dry grass and the creature either dived like a shot or, angry at invasion, savagely grappled with the stalk.

George Steiner has written of the 'paralyzing empathy'[5] evinced by Hofmannsthal's avatar of the impossibility of expression, crystallised in his view of a water beetle set upon its eternal traverse between the edges of a pail:

> Where could you find pity or any comprehensible association of human ideas if on some other evening I find under a nut tree a half-full watering can that a gardener's boy has forgotten there ... and a water beetle sculling on the surface of the water from one dark shore to the other, this confluence of trivialities shoots through me from the roots of my hair to the marrow of my toes with such presence of the infinite that I want to bring out words, knowing that any words I found would vanquish those cherubim in which I do not believe?[6]

Kiely's allusion is real, I believe, and evokes an equally potent sense of ulteriority, albeit a less disabling one. For Hofmannsthal, Chandos embodies an alienation that produces 'a kind of feverish thinking, but thinking in a medium more immediate, more liquid, more glowing, than words'. Kiely's narrator, through a generous, sympathetic divestment – of authority, of priority – that is finally cheerful, cedes his position to his friend. 'I was the stranger,' he reflects, 'who had once been the guide.'

The professor, too, is undergoing a different but related metamorphosis, donning, or revealing, or having awakened within him, his common identity with his forebears, most especially his grandfather, whom he had never known but whose gait he shares, the sign by which he is recognised 'from the top of the Glen' by his grand-uncle, his grandfather's brother. As they ascend and cross the gap into the Glen, the professor's account of his father's memories of *his* father's youth there becomes absorbed into the narrative voice. There is a haunting passage that stands in for and explains a much broader history than might appear on the surface. We are given the young grandfather's view as he crossed the mountain on market day, but the view encompasses a great deal that cannot be seen at all:

> On the tip of one island two tall aerials marked the place where, he was told, messages went down into the sea to travel all the way to America by cable. That was a great marvel for a boy from the mountains to hear about: the ghostly, shrill, undersea voices; the words of people in every tongue of Europe far down among monstrous fish and shapeless sea-serpents that never saw the light of the sun. He closed his eyes one day and it seemed to him that the sounds of the little town were the voices of Europe setting out on their submarine travels. That was the time he knew that when he was old enough he would leave the Glen of Kanareen and go with the voices westwards to America.

This story prefigured Kiely's own journeys to the States, informed and inspired as they were by the notions of the place conjured in his own childhood – G.I.s and purple sage and white wild broncos. It records as well, near to its outset, the importance to him of what grew into a sequence and a cluster of Irish-American friendships that, among their many features, allowed him to stand in welcome to these relatively prosperous but somehow dispossessed voyagers come back from the disacculturating frontiers. At its heart, the story enacts an exchange that occurs with a generosity of spirit so natural as to be almost impersonal, the true custom of the country.

I have said that there is nothing overtly mystical in the story, and even though the word 'ghosts' appears in its final sentence, I would maintain that this is the case, even if credulous readers might still wish to cling piously to the last shreds of scientific materialism. Rather, 'The Dogs in the Great Glen' delves into the realities of inheritance, attachment, morphic resonance, veneration of the dead – in short, knowledge of the primal kind sometimes dismissively referred to as 'folk knowledge'. In a wildly different context and milieu, this understanding is echoed and amplified in a work by the Irish-American writer Harry Mathews in his remarkable novel *Cigarettes*. It is a book not as well known as it should be, so here is a sample from it of what I'm getting at:

I was only beginning to learn that the dead stay everlastingly present among us, taking the form of palpable vacancies that only disappear when, as we must, we take them into ourselves. We take the dead inside us; we fill their voids with our own substance; we become them. The living dead do not belong to a race of fantasy, they constitute the inhabitants of our earth.[7]

The Glen of Kanareen may be difficult to find, yet it also remains constantly available, intimate, accommodating, approachable, an occasion of grounding, rather than the kind of alienated and silencing experience of Chandos. But I'll turn away here from all this richness and leave the professor and the guide, strangers and familiars, there with the dogs approaching and the homecoming still unculminated, and suggest that amid the riches it will provide for any reader, the story was for its author a kind of homecoming gift to a friend, an acknowledgment that, Manhattan islander though he might be, he was most truly at home here in the great Glen of his people, and more so than the man from Omagh.

The story is transmitted, in both directions, along a kind of transatlantic cable, alive with voices departing and returning, out of the past and from distant places. For myself, I'll end merely by saying that it was an honour to know, as a raw youth, all the men mentioned herein. I knew Kevin Sullivan before I read 'The Dogs in the Great Glen' and still now, as with my first reading and, as with, later, so many of the other writings of these eminent friends, I find myself in a kind of indirect interior or ante-room to the story, watching it shift and hover between life and fiction. Tom Flanagan and Ben Kiely both, in quite different ways, mentored me and included me in what seems in distant retrospect more than ever to have been a charmed circle within a vanishing guild. As Ben used to say, referring to the time he met Jack Dempsey, 'Shake the hand that shook the hand.'

THOMAS KILROY

•

'A Dark Writer': The Other Side
of Benedict Kiely

My title comes from the brilliant, radical scholar Liam de Paor, writing in a special issue of *The Recorder* of New York, Summer 1994, celebrating the seventy-fifth birthday of Benedict Kiely. It is worth quoting a passage from de Paor on the subject of Kiely because he anticipates much of what I have to say:

> He is a dark writer, although witty and humorous, accepting as truth but not as justice the way the world is ... Ben remembers Omagh both as it was and as it should have been ... In Carmincross, where nothing happens, Kiely has exploded in one cosmic bang all the bombs together that have torn flesh from bone in more than twenty bloody years in Ulster, and he has shown us how the impotent ravish the virgin bride, as Faulkner does in *Sanctuary*. So again in *Proxopera*. There is an impotent anger at impotence. So it is in much of the world. History is the dark plot in which we must labour, not the sunny hillside across the valley. And Benedict Kiely has done the work.

This is not the version of Kiely with which most people are familiar. He is one of those writers whose warm personality as a man colours his reception as a writer. People who knew and loved that man read the work through this lens of personality, as it were, and this is extremely engaging. The personality is found in the writing largely as a voice, mellifluous, ruminative and stocked with memories, both personal and cultural. The personal emerges in the role of the strolling storyteller. Ben, a convivial centre of every gathering, usually in, or adjacent to, a decent pub. In this sense, Kiely is now recognised as an important figure in the transmission of the Irish oral tradition into a literary form. It is as if he were talking the books into existence. That great talk adds heft to the literary style, shaping the curve of the sentence and the rhythm of the music.

Yet another way of absorbing this style is to say that Kiely, the man and the writer, has a solid foundation in a particular system of values and that this makes up the moral centre of the fiction. Values like comradeship and generosity, decency and respect for others, a rejection of all forms of exploitation, particularly through violence and, always, there is this embracing, capacious sense of humour that appears to be inexhaustible, but not quite. It is a measure of Kiely's stature that the resilience of these values comes under severe pressure when he writes *Proxopera* and *Nothing Happens in Carmincross*. Here one reaches the rage of the man behind the benevolence, the dark writer behind the good company, the sense of tragedy in life below the warmth and goodwill.

It is now generally acknowledged that a change takes place in Kiely's work in 1960 with the publication of *The Captain with the Whiskers*. The landscape is still the familiar one, but now the garden has its serpent. What makes the difference is the figure of the captain. This is a portrayal of evil, an evil that affects the house the captain lives in with his five doomed children, three sons and two daughters, for this is also a novel about the transmission of evil from parent to child, a deadly leakage that touches everything with which it comes into contact, including the house. Captain Chesney dominates the book, although he is dead on the first page. Indeed, part of the book's richness comes from the sophistication of its narrative, particularly its handling of time.

The captain also dominates the consciousness of the young schoolboy Owen Rodgers, as the captain's corrupt daughter Maeve dominates the boy's tortured dreams. Owen learns about evil. This novel is that familiar construction which the Germans call a *Bildungsroman*, a fictional account of the growth towards adulthood of a young man or woman. Owen learns, in de Paor's phrase, 'the way the world is', passing from youth to adulthood. The captain isn't the only influence on Owen. There is also the mentorship of his father, a gentle man of music. Another mentor is the alcoholic priest, Dr Grierson, who embodies Kiely's love of learning. It is significant that the evil of the captain is as important to this process of growth in the boy as is the decent character of the father or the moral presence of the priest:

My father was good and grey, kind and melodious. The captain was a certifiable monster. The doctor was a learned man twisted by celibacy and sustained by drink. It took the three of them to make a man, me, the child of kindness and music, burnt-out hopes and whiskey, and compressed malevolence. That's me. That's man.

The primary sin of the captain is that when he came to establish his house in that sacred Kiely landscape he changed the name of the place from the Irish Magheracolton to the German Bingen, simply as an expression of his own ego. The crime is that of the land-grabber or, given Ulster's particular history, the foreign planter with no respect for the tradition of the locality. This image of a foreign, invading power is extended to the physical description of the captain, a no-necked grotesque in his ridiculous aristocratic tweeds, with his waxed moustache and his sinister, animalistic crouch, settling on his prey.

One of the words Kiely uses to categorise the evil of the captain and the strange allure that he and his family cast over Owen is 'perversion'. When he comes to identify the captain's motivation, Kiely describes the casual cruelty of the sadist: 'the opinions he chose to express at any particular time were always the opinions he knew, with diabolical, uncanny instinct, would offend or hurt his listeners.' Owen wrestles with his fascination with the captain:

Why does he fascinate me, or is it him or the place: the sweep of river, the strand, the black horses, the hard white hills, the sycamores and hazels twisted before constant wind? Was the fascination Bingen or

its owner had for me just the fascination the perverted
thing has for the normal ...?

In passing from *The Captain with the Whiskers* (1960) to
Proxopera (1977) and *Nothing Happens in Carmincross*
(1985), Kiely moves from one sort of evil to another, from
the private to the public sphere, from evil as an internal
force to evil on the street, from the personal to the social,
giving this section of his imaginative life a political edge.
Many of his readers must have been surprised by the
ferocity with which he engaged the mindless slaughter in
his native Ulster in these books. But no reader should have
been so surprised. He was always a man of passionately
held convictions. There is moral indignation in Kiely from
the very beginning of his writing career, often directed
at the social and political absurdities of his native land.
Sometimes the sharpness is muted beneath that rare virtue,
a genuine affection for and tolerance of most human
frailties. When it faces the truly monstrous, as in the legacy
of Captain Chesney, the effect is both chilling and tolerant
– unflinching in its depiction of waste but never losing that
generosity of spirit. Similarly, in facing the horrors recorded
in *Proxopera* and *Nothing Happens in Carmincross*, Kiely
displays a sympathy for the young caught up in violence,
helpless in a kind of innocence or ignorance. Even in the
extremes of violence, Kiely portrays the humanity of his
characters.

These two late books are clearly companion pieces,
separated by years but both dealing with the Northern
Irish Troubles. Yet they are clearly very different kinds
of books. Both are about the moral responsibility of the

bomb and the point at which political activism passes from personal control into a mindless atrocity.

Proxopera is about one of the most unspeakable inventions of the day, the proxy bomb, where a victim is compelled to carry a primed bomb to its destination with members of his family held as hostages until the bomb is in place. The book is a relentless account of what it is like to carry that bomb in that car. Everything is stripped away, leaving that terrifying, sweaty proximity to violent death. A man, alone in a car, with a bomb. The background of the action is suitably economical, 'a well-planted presbyterian countryside', and the style is laconic, terse ('Deliver the goods. That is all you have to do'). The book is, appropriately, shorter than the average novel, more a novella or a long short story, and should be read without interruption. It demands the undivided attention of the reader from start to finish.

In this sense, the work is one of Kiely's least allusive; everything is pared to the bone and there is none of the drifting, comfortable references the reader of Kiely can usually rest on in the reading of the fiction. One of the few references in the book, which is anything but comfortable, is to the 1953 film of Henri-Georges Clouzot, *The Wages of Fear* (*Le Salaire de la Peur*), with Yves Montand in the lead role. It is entirely possible that Kiely learned something about the creation of suspense from this film, with its truckload of nitroglycerine being driven by a desperate driver over the rough mountain roads of a remote South American landscape. I remember the impact the film made when I first saw it in Dublin; precisely the same impact Kiely achieves in *Proxopera*.

Nothing Happens in Carmincross is utterly different in tone to this. Kiely places the horrendous bombing of the town against the rhythms of ordinary life. Something is, indeed, about to happen in Carmincross, something that will mark the place for ever, something in the name of Irish nationalism. Kiely relies here upon the way horror is magnified when it is set in the context of ordinary everyday events. The ferocious irony that holds this disturbing mixture together, the monstrous and the ordinary, begins with the title of the book itself and its mocking negative. Questions tumble through this book, either directly or by implication. None is more urgent than this one: What is heroic about a young woman being blown to bits as she posts invitations to her wedding at a post box in a street of Carmincross?

This brutal treatment of a human body is anticipated early in the book with a kind of black joke: the predicament of the novel's protagonist, Mervyn Kavanagh, travelling in first-class, who finds he has to share space on a transatlantic flight to Shannon with an incontinent man with no legs. The vulnerability of the human body could hardly be revealed more tellingly than this and it is an extraordinary forecast of what is to follow. The writing is a supreme test of the author's tact, given the subject matter of the broken body. Ben Kiely meets the challenge superbly. Details of modern terror stud the narrative of the events that follow. Kiely's expertise as a journalist comes into play as he creates a series of newsflashes that establish, in shocking realism, the nature of a modern terror campaign not only in Ireland but across the globe. This global context matches the suffering of the girl by the post box on the street of Carmincross.

Kiely also establishes the tolerance of the traveller, Mervyn Kavanagh, and the resources of character that he will draw upon to survive the tests to come. Kavanagh becomes a willing carer of the tragic figure beside him on the plane, taking over from the air hostesses the role of nurse of the incontinent man. He is also capable of seeing the black comedy of his own situation in dealing with the helpless man.

On arrival in Ireland, Kavanagh makes a circuitous journey to Carmincross to attend the wedding ('Haste to the wedding and haste to the wedding!') of the doomed girl, his niece. This is one of those familiar Kiely benders or skites, or at least pub-crawls, across the Irish hinterland in agreeable company. It celebrates human fellowship, and is a festival of talk and laughter, stories and songs, of the life-force itself. The friends surrounding Kavanagh on this journey include a useful old pal of his, who happens to be a generous hotel manager called Mr Burns, and a lady called Deborah, who in less guarded times would have been called 'an old flame'. 'A sort of honeymoon, isn't it, astray with a woman on the roads of Ireland.' This particular trip, however, differs from others in the Kiely canon in that, from the beginning, the camaraderie is overshadowed by that broken body from the plane. As the journey goes on, this shadow becomes more pervasive. The litany of horrors grows in detail and the anger of the author increases, allowing him to comment on a variety of issues, including the existential questions, 'What, oh dear Christ, was it all about? What are we doing here?'

Having made the point that these two novels are very different in style and content, it should now be said that, in one crucial respect at least, they share common ground. The protagonists of both books – Kavanagh in *Carmincross* and the father, Binchey, in *Proxopera*, are typical Kiely protagonists. We have met their like before. They are both custodians of tradition. Both are teachers of history. Each has a repository of history that offers a moral measurement of, and a moral commentary on, the action of the books. Each shares Kiely's own ample embrace of this divided community of Northern Ireland, an open generosity that gives both books their weight and stature.

Binchey in *Proxopera* is a retired school teacher whose own family history crosses the sectarian divide. The three IRA men who enter his home come in outlandish costume disguises, like three mummers in a grotesque performance of a tribal ritual. However, ever the acute observer, Binchey, in an ingenious narrative touch, sees through each disguise. He displays the power of knowledge. He recognises one from a family characteristic of the feet and another from the madness of the family eyes. The third he recognises from his accent as an outsider, a displaced Corkman, who is clearly the one in charge of the operation. Kiely is writing about the power that comes from intelligence and imagination, which will prove, in the end, to be greater than the power of bomb or bullet. He is offering, in effect, a radical rereading of Irish history and a redefinition of the heroic.

Mr Binchey drives his car with its lethal cargo into a bog where an explosion can do no harm. When he arrives home, deeply traumatised, he is told: '"You were a hero"', a reversal of the use of that loaded word. In *Nothing Happens in Carmincross* the word heroism is similarly subjected to probing through the graphic descriptions of the destruction of innocent people by bombing. A whole tradition of the use of physical force for political ends is held up to scrutiny.

The heroic myth of physical force is central to one reading of Irish history. The specific problem facing Kiely in these novels is that the record of this myth is preserved in two versions of writing, both of which have a particular appeal to Kiely himself. He loved this material. You could say that he dedicated a good portion of his life to its legacy. One version is to be found in poetry, best seen in the example of Yeats, who aestheticises violence in the cold image of Cúchulainn in the General Post Office, a single image that led Yeats in many different, complex directions. The second, more important at a personal level to Kiely, is the physical force tradition that survives in words and music in the vast, popular collection of Irish lore of which Kiely was an expert exponent and performer. There is an elegiac mood in the songs and poems of these two novels. At one point there is even a sad acknowledgment that the words of the ballads may now have to be changed.

Towards the end of the second novel, Kiely turns to Yeats with another ironic twist. This is Yeats at his most romantic, the Yeats of the Innisfree lake, and Kiely merges this romantic lake, in a daring sleight, with his own lake of Carmincross. One picture feeds the other. This Carmincross lake is now no lake of romantic, poetic reverie but a lake of death (the local lake in *Proxopera* has similarly been blighted by terroristic outrage, giving rise to Binchey's refrain as he drives his weapon, 'The lake will never be the same'). The romantic image of the hero is forced to respond to the reality of what slaughter means. The whole passage in *Nothing Happens in Carmincross* is laced with the militaristic jingles of Sir Henry Newbolt, the laureate of the late British Empire. Imperialistic bravado is called upon in support of militaristic Irish nationalism. Imperial jingoism is seen to have the same militaristic appeal as traditional Irish ballads:

> And in silence in the hills somewhere above Carmincross, perhaps by the shore of that quiet lake, water lapping with low sound and all that, the killers mixed their ingredients on the previous night. And their cars were manned in silence and in silence pulled away and in silence every gunner took his post ... With a volley from their broadsides the citadel they shook and they hammered back like heroes all the night. A lady who was watching a television programme called *Watch with Mother* was the first to hear the heavenly cars descending from the hills. The swishing of their tyres was distinct. She thought it was the army. She called her husband. He looked out the window. He saw the cars. He knew they meant no good.

THOMAS O'GRADY

•

The Treacherous Waves of Lough Muck: A Hypertextual Reading of *Proxopera*

In subject matter and theme, Benedict Kiely's novella *Proxopera* is one of the most important works of fiction to emerge from the so-called Troubles that scourged Northern Ireland from the late 1960s through the late 1990s. Published in 1977, the narrative speaks out bravely against the bombing campaign directed against the British presence in the North by the nationalist Irish Republican Army. Exposing both the ruthlessness and the shallowness of a trio of terrorists (ostensibly IRA, though not explicitly named as such) who hold a family captive in their home at the edge of a small lake in the Northern Irish countryside, the story at the heart of the novella is very simple. A retired schoolteacher, Mr Binchey, is instructed by the captors, under threat of harm to his family – his son and daughter-in-law, their two children and their housekeeper – to deliver to the nearby town a bomb packed inside a creamery can. En route to complete this 'proxy operation', Mr Binchey articulates his dilemma explicitly: 'I drive on, sick with fear and an awful resignation, to bring death to my own, to keep death from my own.'[1] The embodiment of high moral rectitude, Mr Binchey ultimately abandons his car in a bog, where the bomb detonates. His town is spared, and even his family escapes relatively unscathed – his son is kneecapped, and the family home is set on fire by the retreating terrorists, though not completely destroyed. The narrative ends with Mr Binchey, surrounded by his family and his loyal housekeeper, lying in a hospital bed and remembering how in his boyhood he coveted the white house on a lake that eventually did become his own home, which has also become an emblem of the innocence that the practitioners of sectarian violence would wantonly destroy: 'And the most beautiful thing of all, cutting across a corner of the lawn, a small brook tumbling down to join the lake. To have your own stream on your own lawn is the height of everything.' (93)

Yet, the simplicity of such a synopsis belies first of all the thematic complexity of what is truly at stake in *Proxopera*. Distinguishing between story and plot, E.M. Forster observes: 'We have defined a story as a narrative of events arranged in their time-sequence. A plot is also a narrative of events, the emphasis falling on causality.'[2] In an afterword written for an American edition of the novella, Kiely reveals that the original for his Mr Binchey was one Michael J. Curry, a beloved teacher of 'Latin and English literature in the High, or Secondary, school that was honoured by my attendance'[3] in his hometown of Omagh, County Tyrone. Recalling Curry's righteous rejection of the nationalist paramilitary violence of the 1920s – the period of the Irish War of Independence against British rule and then the Irish Civil War – Kiely endows Mr Binchey with a similar righteousness. But holding true to the writerly strategy he practised throughout his long and prolific career – 'You pick a bit from here and a bit from there'[4] – Kiely complicates Curry's principled stand by deeply implicating his protagonist personally in what unfolds in the narrative:

> [I]t seemed to me an obvious, perhaps too obvious, ploy to place M.J. Curry in the middle of one of our unhappy contemporary situations and try to imagine how he might react. For the sake of the story I had given him what you might call a false or another identity and background: an ancestry in the town, a son and grandchildren, a white house by a lake.[5]

The plot of *Proxopera* is thus driven forward by the immediacy of Mr Binchey's grappling with the dire consequences for his family of his failing to complete the proxy operation versus the consequences of his carrying out his orders, which would result in random deaths and widespread destruction in his beloved hometown. The plot certainly thickens the basic story line.

Ultimately, however, the enduringness of *Proxopera* rests not just on the bold transparency of its central theme and the complications of its plot but even more so on a bravura narrative style that, while also belying the relative simplicity of the novella's story, ultimately locates *Proxopera*, in literary terms, among the most ambitious and the most accomplished of all Kiely's many fictional narratives. The unsuspecting reader is introduced to that style in the opening sentence, in the form of a decontextualised quotation that turns out to be from a comic ballad of decidedly local origins: '*Sea-lions and sharks, alligators and whales with mouths that would swallow a truck ...*' (9). That sentence is followed by a similarly decontextualised reference to a lake, then by another line from the ballad, and then by a decontextualised reference to the Nazi concentration camp at Dachau. Eventually Mr Binchey will reveal that the ballad was written by '[a] man I know' (30), and readers acquainted with Benedict Kiely's work and life might recognise that the fictional Mr Binchey is referring to the real-life author of 'The Treacherous Waves of Lough Muck', Frank McCrory, who happens also to be Kiely's brother-in-law.[6] By that time – probably long before then – the alert reader will also have recognised that the narrative strategy deployed by Kiely in *Proxopera*, establishing Mr Binchey as the 'center of consciousness' for the entire novella, is strikingly reminiscent of that deployed by James Joyce in the foundational first six episodes of *Ulysses*.

INTERIOR MONOLOGUE AND HYPERTEXTUALITY

Joyce himself described his narrative strategy – or 'technic'– for those episodes, which introduce Stephen Dedalus and Leopold Bloom to his readers, as a combination of 'dialogue', 'narration' and 'soliloquy' which allows the author to move seamlessly between the inner and the outer lives of his characters.[7] Obviously, dialogue and third-person narration are staples of literary storytelling. But, especially for first-time readers of Joyce, the narrative style that he labelled 'soliloquy' can be disorienting. Now more commonly known as 'interior monologue', this style attains its extreme form as 'stream of consciousness' – essentially interior monologue without any filtering intrusion on the part of the author – in Molly Bloom's musings in the 'Penelope' episode of *Ulysses*, eight 'sentences' that weave and unweave themselves over the final thirty-five pages of the novel. But Stephen Dedalus's interior monologue opening the third episode of the novel, 'Proteus', is a more pertinent example for Kiely's channelling of Joyce in *Proxopera*:

> Ineluctable modality of the visible: at least that if no more, thought through my eyes. Signatures of all things I am here to read: seaspawn and seawrack, the nearing tide, that rusty boot. Snotgreen, bluesilver, rust: coloured signs. Limits of the diaphane. But he adds: in bodies. Then he was aware of them bodies before of them coloured. How? By knocking his sconce against them, sure. Go easy. Bald he was and a millionaire, *maestro di color che sanno*.[8]

If the reader can recognise that the final phrase, in Italian, is Dante's description of Aristotle – 'master of those who know' – and then re-reads the passage, it can be paraphrased simply enough as Stephen's musing on the challenges a literary artist faces when attempting to inscribe the complexity of human experience as described by Aristotle (and others).[9]

Mr Binchey's interior monologue is also dense with what may seem, at first, arcane references. Some of these, like recurring snippets from 'The Treacherous Waves of

Lough Muck' – and like many of the references that contribute to the narrative texture of *Ulysses* – are easily glossed. His musing, for example, on 'what people thought long ago, they called rivers after goddesses' (10) needs to be understood in terms of the ancient *dinnseanchas* tradition of place-naming in Ireland.[10] In a different way, Mr Binchey's remembering how a fresh-water spring in a rock face had been, for his boyhood self, 'the well at the world's end' (11) directs the reader toward a fantasy novel of that title published in 1896 by William Morris. References to an Orange Hall and then to Orangemen and William of Orange and the Battle of the Boyne and its commemoration every year in July may not even require glossing for most readers of a narrative set in Northern Ireland. But Mr Binchey's reflections on the giant Lambeg drums beaten 'with bamboo canes by sweating coatless men with bleeding knuckles' leads him, and the reader, to two musings that resonate not only each unto itself but also with implications for the entire narrative of *Proxopera*.

The first of these – 'Odd as the jungle it all was, bongo, bongo, bongo, I don't want to leave the Congo!' (13) – may seem at a glance to be just an incidental nod by Mr Binchey toward 'Civilization', a jazz tune recorded in 1947 by the Woody Herman Orchestra. The second musing involves his envisioning members of the Orange Lodge marching in their annual parades that culminate on 12 July: 'On the silken picture-banners King William on a white horse went splashing across the Boyne, or Queen Victoria sat on a throne and handed a bible to a kneeling negress and the legend said: The secret of England's greatness' (13). A ready reader will recognise that *The Secret of England's Greatness* is the title of an iconic painting by Thomas Jones Barker housed in the National Portrait Gallery in London. Painted in 1863, it is clearly an overt emblematising of British imperialism, an unabashed licensing of the culture of Unionist religious bigotry and oppression that permeates the North and which thus fuels the sectarian violence that propels the plot of *Proxopera*.

What these two disparate musings have in common is how they reveal to the reader, very early in the novel – tellingly, even before the Binchey family is taken hostage – both the impressive range of Mr Binchey's knowledge and the associational way that his mind works. In his afterword for the American edition of *Proxopera*, Kiely himself draws attention to these qualities in his protagonist, noting that he added history to Mr Binchey's M.J. Curry-inspired literature-centred teaching portfolio; and as the plot unfolds, the reader begins to recognise how crucial Mr Binchey's knowledge of history – specifically the linked histories of Ireland and England – is to the deep resonance of the novella that, again, extends far beyond its simple story. For close to a century, committed readers of James Joyce have enhanced their engagement with *Ulysses* by tracing the countless extra-textual references that give that novel the distinctively dense narrative texture that makes it what Joyce himself called 'my damned monster-novel'.[11]

Almost thirty years ago, Jay David Bolter, a scholar of media and technology, recognised the possibilities of mining, via electronic links on the still-evolving internet, the allusive richness of both *Ulysses* and *Finnegans Wake*, which he labelled 'hypertexts that have been flattened out to fit on the printed page'.[12] A decade later Joyce scholar Michael Groden formally proposed an electronic edition of *Ulysses*.[13] While that project got derailed by copyright claims made by the Joyce estate, as recently as 2015 Amanda Visconti defended her doctoral dissertation at the University of Maryland in which she apparently modelled an updated version of what Groden had proposed. Obviously, *Proxopera* is written on a much smaller scale than *Ulysses*. Yet, by virtue of Kiely's masterful deployment of that narrative strategy derived from Joyce, the reader is encouraged to read the novella as a vital example of what Professor George Landow described as an '*implicit* hypertext in nonelectronic form'.[14] Indeed, for the reader pausing to identify and to reflect on the vast number of allusions and other extra-textual references that emerge from Mr Binchey's interior monologue – in effect, to undertake a hypertextual reading of the narrative – the reward is more than commensurate with the length of the novella.

LET ME CARRY YOUR CROSS FOR IRELAND, LORD

There is hardly a paragraph in *Proxopera* that does not give the reader pause over some word or phrase or expression that reaches outside or beyond the text. Some of these arise naturally from the social or linguistic landscape of the narrative: 'turbary' (17) refers to the rights to dig turf in a peat bog; housekeeper Minnie's contemptuous reference to 'the Coldcream Gurkhas' (21) wittily elides two British Army regiments – the Coldstream Guards and the Ghurka Regiment – in an intentional malapropism; Mr Binchey's musing on 'Caithlin Ni Houlihan, the Hag of Beare and Caith Ni Dhuibhir' (66) reminds the reader of the conventional feminising personification of Ireland dating back to the time of the Penal Laws in the eighteenth century; and his reflection on how 'close to Newry town the UVF or was it the UDA murdered a showband' (68) refers to the ambush, on 31 July 1975, of the popular Miami Showband by members of the Ulster Volunteer Force, a loyalist paramilitary group (which included members of the British Army's Ulster Defence Regiment) at Buskhill, Co. Down. Other references emerge specifically from the literary dimensions of Mr Binchey's teaching career. These allusions include passages from Catullus (35); Charlotte Elizabeth's 'The Maiden City' (38); Edmund Spenser's *A View of the State of Ireland* (40); Charles Dickens's *The Old Curiosity Shop* (41); Rudyard Kipling's poems 'A Smuggler's Song' (43–44) and 'Boots' (93); Donagh MacDonagh's 'Going to Mass Last Sunday' (61–62); Douglas Hyde's 'Ringleted Youth of My Love' (62); Thomas Hood's 'Miss Kilmansegg and Her Precious Leg' (76); Thomas Otway's play *Venice Preserv'd* (84); Robert Louis Stevenson's 'Requiem' (85) and Tennyson's 'Passing of Arthur' from *Idylls of the King* (85).

A more elaborate reference, however, to the movie *The Battle of Britain* (1969) exemplifies how deeply a hypertextual reading can complicate the simple story at the heart of *Proxopera*. One of the captors is watching the movie on the television when Mr Binchey and his family enter their home.

Against a blue sky a fighter-plane is falling, twisting, leaving behind it a spiral of black smoke. The battle of Britain. Then he sees Minnie, stiff as a stick in a high wooden armchair. Gagged and bound. In a rough Belfast accent the third man says: Wizard prangs. And the bastards of Brits wouldn't even give us the credit for Paddy Finnucane. They say no Irishman was killed in the Battle of Britain. (20)

Aside from the expression 'Wizard prangs' – English slang for 'impressive crashes' – these few sentences demand more than a simple gloss. Obviously, the very title of the film resonates with the centuries-old political tension between Ireland and Britain. But beyond that, Mr Binchey, as a teacher of history, would know the importance in the British public imagination of the actual battle, a protracted engagement between the Royal Air Force and the Luftwaffe, involving both bombers and fighter planes, from July through October 1940. The campaign's significance was predicted by Winston Churchill in a House of Commons speech given on 18 June, more than three weeks before the battle began:

What General Weygand called the Battle of France is over. I expect that the battle of Britain is about to begin. Upon this battle depends the survival of Christian civilization. Upon it depends our own British life and the long continuity of our institutions and our Empire … Let us therefore brace ourselves to our duties, and so bear ourselves that, if the British Empire and its Commonwealth last for a thousand years, men will still say, 'This was their finest hour'.[15]

Like so many of Churchill's speeches throughout his long career as statesman, this one, with its pointed rhetoric – 'Christian civilization', 'our own British life', 'our Empire', 'their finest hour' – was crafted not only to inspire in the moment but also to endure 'for a thousand years' as a statement of British imperial values. The film drama was made accordingly. Featuring many icons of British stage and screen – Sir Laurence Olivier, Trevor Howard, Michael Caine, Christopher Plummer and Robert Shaw, among them – it plays as a vehicle not just of historical record but also of British triumphalism. Mr Binchey would know all this. His television-watching captor, however, reveals his shallow provincialism by pouting over the failure of the movie to give due to Irish-born RAF fighter pilot Paddy Finnucane, who was indeed a hero of the battle yet whose story obviously does not fit with the overarching intention of the movie. Ironically, the ringleader of the proxy operation recognises his comrade's shallowness: 'Soldier-boy on your feet. You stupid fucker. The Battle of Britain and Paddy Finnucane' (55).

But the moment in *Proxopera* that perhaps best illustrates Kiely's stylistic confluence with James Joyce and *Ulysses* – and, incidentally, his thematic confluence too – occurs, tellingly, at the juncture in the narrative when Mr Binchey embarks on his freighted mission and his mind begins to race to the pace of the ticking bomb. In a matter of three paragraphs (56–59) Kiely unlooses through Mr Binchey's interior monologue a veritable cascade of deeply resonant allusions that the dedicated reader would be well-rewarded to treat as '*implicit* hypertext in nonelectronic form'. The cascade begins with Mr Binchey seeing in his handcuffed son an image from William Cullen Bryant's poem 'The African Chief': 'His son stands silent, chained in the market-place amid the gathering multitude that shrank to hear his name'. This then segues, via the nationalist mantra 'Ireland Gaelic and free', to lines from T.D. Sullivan's ballad 'God Save Ireland', written in 1867 to commemorate the Manchester Martyrs, a trio of Irish nationalists hanged in England for their role (purported) in abetting the escape from prison of two Fenians: 'never till the latest day shall the memory pass away of the gallant lives thus given for our land'. And that in turn segues – this is all in one long sentence – to a phrase from a common Orange Order toast that would have Ulster 'safe from popery and brass money and wooden shoes'. From there, Mr Binchey's mind leaps to A.E. Houseman's poem 'Bredon Hill' – 'Come all to church, good people;/Good people come and pray' – and then to a generic 'angel of death' linked to the phrase 'on the wing', probably from Edward Fitzgerald's 'The Rubaiyat of Omar Khayyam', before ending with 'ye know neither the day nor the hour' from the Gospel of Matthew (25:13).

The second paragraph of this passage opens with Mr Binchey glancing toward Henry Wadsworth Longfellow's poem 'The Slave's Dream' (evidently prompted by his prior recollection of Bryant's poem on a similar subject): 'Before him like a blood-red flag the bright flamingoes flew'. Then, triggered by the thought of his wife buried in a churchyard he will pass with his ticking bomb, Mr Binchey recalls a line from W.B. Yeats's poem 'Lullaby': 'Beloved, may your sleep be sound'. But then, self-consciously aware of the load he is carrying in the boot of his car – 'Death sleeps in the silver can' – he remembers a movie he saw with his wife in Dublin, *The Wages of Fear* (1953). Based on a novel *Le salaire de la peur* by Georges Arnaud (*né* Henri Girard), the film dramatises the predicament of four desperate European expatriates hired to drive two trucks of nitroglycerine over treacherous mountain roads in Venezuela. For Mr Binchey – and thus for the reader – the analogy with his predicament is transparent: 'a blinding flash over the ridge, scarcely an explosion, just a blinding flash and that was that'.

Yet, for Mr Binchey the analogy breaks down in his observing how 'at least those wrecks of men were paid to carry the stuff'. And that distinction brings his cascading thoughts into focus on the precise nature of the enterprise he has been forced to participate in: 'the proxy bomb, operation proxy, proxopera for gallant Irish patriots fighting imaginary empires by murdering the neighbours'. Having reflected further on lines from T.D. Sullivan's 'God Save Ireland', its incendiary rhetoric no less pointed than Winston Churchill's speeches almost seventy-five years later, he feels his righteous anger rising: 'And on the cause must go, through joy or weal or woe, till we make Ireland a nation free and grand.' His indignation intensifying, he thinks next of Yeats's excited rhetoric surrounding the Easter Rising of 1916, eliding lines from his late poem 'The Statues' and 'September 1913': 'Could Pearse in the post office have, by proxy, summoned Cuchulain to his side, could the wild geese have, by proxy, spread the grey wing on the bitter tide, could all that delirium of the brave not have died by proxy, Edward Fitzgerald, and Robert Emmet and Wolfe Tone?'

Arguably, however, the pivotal moment of *Proxopera* with regard to hypertextuality occurs when Mr Binchey notes that the ringleader of the captors, whom he dubbed Corkman because of his accent, 'seemed semi-educated, and must know that poem, and also, let me carry your cross for Ireland, Lord, but let some other unfortunate fucker carry the bomb for me'. Less widely known than the Yeats and Sullivan poems, 'Let Me Carry Your Cross for Ireland, Lord', by Thomas Ashe, a cultural and militant nationalist who commanded a battalion during the Easter Rising and subsequently died of mistreatment during a hunger strike at Mountjoy Prison in 1917, emblematises the value of reading *Proxopera* as a hypertext that has been 'flattened out to fit on the printed page'. Obviously, Mr Binchey knows the poem, with its lofty religion-infused nationalism and its idealising of martyrdom for the cause of Ireland, and he assumes that Corkman does too. And so does Benedict Kiely assume that his reader will either know the poem or, more likely, will make a point of knowing it.

For clearly, just as Mr Binchey's perspective on the world, conveyed to the reader through Joycean interior monologue, is shaped by the broadness of his knowledge of literature and of history – and of his awareness of literature *as* history – so is Corkman's shaped by narrowness: 'let me carry your cross for Ireland, Lord', indeed. That is the sort of narrowness that 'enslaves' not only others – like Mr Binchey's son – but also the self. It is the same narrowness that infuses both 'God Save Ireland' and that Orange Order toast to 'the glorious, pious and immortal memory of the great and good King William'.

In that regard, as a 'hypertextual' reading of that casual reference to Ashe's poem reveals, the poem carries the weight of history that prescribes the culture of sectarian intolerance and paramilitary violence that the narrative inscribes. Late in the narrative, Mr Binchey's housekeeper asks him: 'Who guided them or misguided them?' His reply is telling: 'Ireland. A long history. England. Empire. King William. The Pope. Ian Paisley. Myself. I was a teacher of history' (84).

The short concluding section of *Proxopera* begins with Mr Binchey waking in his hospital bed and seething inwardly: 'But by the living Jesus they should not have touched my house, my living dream seen across water and through tall reeds and beech trees ...' (91). It is no mere coincidence that Kiely's next-published work of long fiction, *Nothing Happens in Carmincross* (1985), has as its lead epigraph a wistful longing that James Joyce expresses through his character Stephen Dedalus in *Ulysses*: 'History is a nightmare from which I am trying to awake'.[16]

COLUM MCCANN

•

Seanchaí and Silence

Long ago and far away, my father gave me the short story 'A Ball of Malt and Madame Butterfly' to read. I was sixteen years old, slouching through Dublin, feigning an adolescent literary swagger. At the time I was fiercely into the American Beat writers – Kerouac, Ginsberg, Snyder, Ferlinghetti – and thought nobody could touch them. I couldn't quite get my head around the idea of Irish fiction. It was the sort of stuff decorated, surely, with teacups and lace curtains. I was influenced, no doubt, by my Inter Cert reading which, incidentally, was more about Maupassant than anyone else. The idea of Irish writing didn't figure for me yet. No Joyce. No Beckett. No O'Brien. I began the Kiely story with a scowl, but soon enough I loosened into it. I wasn't quite sure what I had encountered, but, a few pages in, the oxygen was gone from the air. I was knocked off my smug balance. I needed more. I entered the Kiely world at that very moment, and within months I had read all of it from beginning to end. And then one day I called Ben Kiely (we had a connection through my father, Seán, features editor of the *Evening Press*), and he invited me into his home in Donnybrook. We shared a ball of malt.

No Madame Butterfly. No matter. She was already alive in my imagination.

There are certain voices that come along and make the claim that nobody should forget and – even more radically – that nobody should be forgotten. These voices remind us that life is not yet written down: there is so much more left to happen. They are led by delight that the world is varied and ongoing. The true value of literature is that there's always another story to tell. Ben Kiely is one hundred years here. I mark so much of the Irish literary adventure in both the twentieth and twenty-first centuries by my sip of that first ball of malt.

The work of any writer is concerned with the doings of his fellow men and women with whom he shares some territory, some rage, a little loss and maybe even some faith. He doesn't speak for them, but with them. Of all the Irish writers of the past century, perhaps Ben Kiely has been one of the closest to the voices of the people about whom he wrote – the journalists, the farmers, the tradesmen, the publicans, the firemen, the hookers – yes, even *the hoors on the half-doors* – and countless others who make up the bric-a-brac of our lives.

Kiely was well aware that there were many ways of living besides his own. He found value in that which others left as useless. Only someone who listened well could have produced the stories he told. He could sing and shout with the best of them. He could also haul a laugh out of the darkest corners. He saw malice as another name for mediocrity. He spoke the truth in wild, gabby, discursive ways. He had a great affection for the anecdote, the song, the scrap of local verse that brought a wakeful grace to the language of ordinary people. And, most importantly of all, he understood the interior clockwork of those same people. He was there when the bread came out of the oven. There were no damp white loaves in his work. He got things fresh.

It is possible, of course, to over-saint our writers when they are gone. Too little too late, perhaps. Kiely, in his day, was recognised internationally – on the front page of the *New York Times Book Review*, for instance, where, reviewing the compilation of stories entitled *The State of Ireland*, Guy Davenport wrote, 'The first meaning of "the state of Ireland" is that it's a place where stories are still told, deliciously and by masters of the art, of whom Benedict Kiely is one, perhaps the foremost.' Confirmed modernist though he was, Davenport also happened to take the view that 'art is always a replacement of indifference by attention', a statement that might have been written in praise of Kiely, just as the title of Davenport's most substantial book, *The Geography of the Imagination*, could be taken as a signpost to his imaginative magic and method. Yet, regardless of such high-quality and oft-repeated critical recognition (by such fellow artists as John Updike, William Kennedy, Thomas Flanagan and Anthony Burgess, among others), and despite Kiely's election to the position of Saoi in Aosdána, we have somehow allowed him to slip between the floorboards of what we thought was new and what we reckoned was old. A perverse monism lingers, insisting that Kiely should have been read only if you're white, Irish and over fifty. The truth is, of course, that Kiely should be read in Brixton. He should be read in Mississippi. He should be read in Neilstown.

Though he stayed at home (apart from his forays down along Peachtree), he was one of the international brigade.

Sometimes – for his sins – Ben got labelled a *seanchaí*. It shouldn't be a curse word, but in contemporary Ireland it has, over the years, lent an unfortunate air of Grey Eminence to his work, as if his themes and concerns had suddenly become *passé*. But any taint of 'come-all-ye' rust that's said to be around his writing is perversely misleading. It's almost like being mistreated in the nicest possible way. Somehow there was a disingenuous idea that Kiely was a traditional, or entrenched, writer. Nothing in fact could be further from the truth. But he never had big film advances. No Booker Prizes. No medals of honour, unless the 'national literary award' of having three of his novels banned by the Irish Censorship Board counts. Kiely kept quiet about that. There was a grace about his silence. He proceeded from a reckless inner need. He knew that truth threatened power. He worked beyond the constraints of the Catholic Church. He put the boot in, but he didn't sing about the bruises.

The sense of Ben Kiely as the Grey Irish Eminence was developed primarily in the early 1990s and the raw years of the new century. The desire to label him might have been a desire to embalm him, to hold on to a little slice of old Ireland. It was benevolent and celebratory and genuine in its affection, but even a compliment can dig ditches. Being a Grey Eminence surely isn't all it's cracked up to be. Robert Frost, for one, didn't entirely benefit when the American academy stuck the label on him. All the photographs of Frost captured him at a certain age, with a certain look in his eye, wearing a certain grey suit, in a certain grey landscape. Frost was pickled in aspic, as Kiely often was towards the end of his years. Both became the figure of the benign old man, the kindly father of a certain sort of poetics, the sort of man to whom you might entrust your metaphors in case they went astray. It wasn't that Frost had even journeyed on a road less travelled; he had gotten there, to the end of the road, and the journey was considered largely irrelevant. To critics, readers and authors, the important thing was the fact that Frost had *arrived*. As a consequence, he was suddenly a man who had been old even when he was young. People stopped reading his poems, feeling they had no need to since they *knew* Frost so intimately already. He was immediately cobwebbed into a different time, an older time, more secure, less offensive. His innovations were somehow seen as quaint. In effect, he was housebroken. It took a long time and a lot of righteous anger to free Frost from the grips of an essentially well-meaning compliment.

Something not too far from this happened to Kiely – he was placed in the dictionary between *seanchaí* and silence. Kiely was either somebody who was looking after old Ireland, or somebody whom new Ireland was to be embarrassed by. Sure, he had an old-fashioned delight in narrative and character, but he was pigeon-holed as a writer of 'older' stories; to be taken as a 'quiet' author; to be seen in a 'conservative' context; or to be stuffed into the 'quintessentially Irish' box. Somehow, there was a perception that it was all about peasants, emigrants, farm-boys and other sundry embarrassments. The people who didn't read his stories were the ones who were loudest about his stasis. They believed that Kiely's writing operated in an Ireland for which they had already developed a nostalgia. I am acquainted with plenty of young writers who knew the name Ben Kiely. They even invoked him in interviews or onstage. But the name bobbed up like a Hallowe'en apple, and was quickly submerged. Their loss. Ours too. Kiely was – indeed is – one of our great writers, one of our most contemporary and one of our most profound. His early work is surely equal to that of Seán O'Faoláin and Frank O'Connor. His later novels put him in a realm of his own, not least for being among the few to go to the actual pulse of the wound known as the Troubles. In these works Kiely reveals his knowledge of the poison of narrow lives, and where empathy could trump it. In *Proxopera* it is not Yeats's ceremony of innocence that is drowned but a ceremony of evil. And *Nothing Happens in Carmincross* – a novel of the many forms of loss, not least both exile and the wreckage of home – should be on every Irish bookshelf. When an extended history of the Troubles comes to be written, these novels will be vital. While unpretentious and effortless, they are also a triumph of literary compression. They have a tremendous ability to interpret the everyday temperature of life, and yet also examine the awful heat of hatred.

As much as the late McGahern, Kiely has made the past durable and, at the same time, the present possible. Over the sixty years of his writing, he has been both the thorn and the salve. The wounds he has inflicted, then repaired, are not to be forgotten. Kiely was consistently innovative, powerful and subversive. In terms of the construction and power of his short stories, he is a writer who stands shoulder to shoulder not just with the Irish masters of the form but also with the Russians and the French. When critiquing a writer it is possible to fall into a sort of perverse literary Olympics. Still, the names come from all corners of the globe. Tolstoy, Joyce, Balzac, Márquez, Hemingway. A good story operates in the world as a sort of scaffolding to our souls, not as an event for flags. The benevolent restrictions placed on Kiely are not helped by the fact that he was preceded in his own country by O'Faoláin, O'Flaherty, Joyce, Frank O'Connor, Mary Lavin and McGahern. Readers believe that they know what an Irish short story *is* and how it should conduct itself in the world. So it is with Russian stories, French stories, even the contemporary American short story, as if a national voice is somehow coded in the DNA. And yet it is appropriate to argue that Kiely's stories operate beyond their accepted borders in a sort of international sphere, where he stands side by side with all the aforementioned greats, whose work is interpreted not only nationally but also as a key to what William Faulkner calls 'the intricacies of the human heart'. Indeed. Rack one up for complexity.

Kiely's range of reference and his literary adventurousness do not announce themselves or call undue attention to the role they play in his stories. That he is one of the most erudite and informed writers of recent times is not in doubt, but the stories are never diseased with self-consciousness. He has absorbed the great works, and is at ease in a variety of contexts and literary companions (Balzac, Oregon, *Finnegans Wake*, theology, pop culture), and yet he is essentially rooted in the calm of his own voice. Take that classic story 'A Ball of Malt and Madame Butterfly'. It is a tale of a half-Japanese Dubliner, Madame

Butterfly, 'a young woman of questionable virginity', who plies her trade in The Dark Cow pub along the quays. The narrator, a newspaperman, tells the story of how a civil servant, Pike Hunter, falls in love with her, pursues her, loses her and, in the process, his mind. There is a remarkable range of literary references and allusions in the story, including Synge, Joyce, Spenser, Maupassant, Gilbert and Sullivan, W.B. Yeats and Maud Gonne (both of whom are also among the story's characters). Oblique literary references resound throughout, yet when Pike starts regaling Madame Butterfly with obscure Yeatsian love poems, she turns around to say that Pike would 'puke you with poethry'.

Language, of all the mediums we use, is the most volatile and unyielding, and therefore the most difficult to make memorable. Kiely, rather than stripping language down, layers it, so that it becomes a resonant, hypnotic chant. The sense of movement upon movement, digression into digression, song piled onto song, is overwhelming in its intensity and warmth, creating a home for the reader, any reader, within the story. In the manner of Joyce, Kiely's stories are beautifully laced through with songs, ballads, myths and colloquialisms, all of which are often reappropriated and twisted, operating in a new sphere, bumping up against their old meanings. As in all great work, this creates a number of levels in the stories. The layers and levels of narration in any given story are stunning, and yet the architecture is seemingly simple. This gift for fluent ease is the ultimate in difficulty.

One of the things that Kiely knew so well was that everybody – even the most anonymous amongst us – is in the midst of the story. Our lives don't begin or end: they continue. Nobody achieves perfect serenity. The comfort we gain from death is that life itself is a delight, and that the hard truth of leaving is nothing in comparison to having been around.

In the course of his long writing career there was much that concerned Kiely – issues of sexuality, nationhood, secrecy, the inability to return home – but he also got to the sundry sorrows of violence. When on 15 August 1998, a bomb ripped through Omagh town, claiming twenty-nine lives, it just so happened that it was Kiely's seventy-ninth birthday. But the acute sorrow that befell the town had been written by Kiely before. In the words of John Montague, Kiely had, over the years, seen 'substantial things hustled into oblivion'. Metaphorically, Kiely had had his hands in the dark pockets of a divided country since his earliest fiction, including, but certainly not limited to, 'The Night We Rode with Sarsfield', 'Bluebell Meadow' and 'Down then by Derry'. There inheres in Kiely's work a sense of astonished being, even in the face of death. And in many ways, he was able to foresee, or at least dream, an Ireland without bombs going off in supermarkets, or thumbs hitching a lift to heaven or hell.

What consistently sets his outrage apart, and made it real, was Kiely's deep, enduring love for the landscape and the people. They are good people. They are funny. They laugh. They tell stories. They fall in and out of love. Occasionally they are left at an age where they will never grow any older. This slice of joy amid the sorrow is the key to Kiely's genius. The stories are always lyrical, allusive, digressive and full of unavoidable happiness, even colossal jokes. '"… once upon a time I laughed easily,"' says the narrator of 'Down then by Derry'. '"It was easy to laugh here then."'

And let it not be forgotten that Kiely was one of the funniest writers that this country produced. Sometimes the humour was in the deep knowledge, sometimes it was in the sadness, but at other times it was right there on the page, apparent, drawing attention to itself, waiting to be laughed at. Colossal extended jokes. Hidden jibes at fellow newspapermen. The lines of songs repeated endlessly and changed, and resung. The snippets of old poems turned around. Kiely could make you laugh out loud. Madame Butterfly being hauled back from the window and her 'lover' climbing out first. The plump girl in (and out) of her jodhpurs in 'A Letter to Peachtree'. Gasmask's snores, which 'ride on like advancing shingly waves' in *Proxopera*. The refrain of 'Them's your cats … them's your pigeons' in 'Bloodless Byrne of a Monday'. The fish singing along the banks of the River Strule. In 'Down then by Derry', a medical officer organises a sports day in the local lunatic asylum, a bicyclist is catapulted among the lunatic ladies, the birds make mocking calls among the hidden lovers' lanes, Tennyson is judged to have something awry with his bowels, Milton is considered a bit of a bore, a lazy policeman sits all day on the courthouse steps, murders in America are seen to be picturesque, bulls are celebrated for their endowments, nuns chase young boys through the rain, and yet the accumulated lightness of the story highlights the ache, the grief and the serious loss of another time. That acute Kiely sense of being alive, again. His tales are never written in abstraction. On the contrary, it's as if he reaches into our bodies, touching the funny-bone while at the same time wrenching our hearts a notch backwards. Our Gogol. Our Gorky. Our Balzac. Our Faulkner. He gave the world a democratic welcome.

There is often a temptation with the celebration of a life – but especially a significant life – to lament the loss of a generation. There goes McGahern. There goes Heaney. There goes Montague. There went Ben Kiely. It is as if all of a sudden the stopping clocks agree – there goes, and went, Old Ireland too. But the only way to counter such doom – the only way to keep these voices alive – is to read the work. Ashes don't return to wood, but to paper they just might.

Stories about him will be told for ever: in pubs, on stone bridges, in train stations, at swinging gates, by firesides, along the banks of his hometown 'serpentine Strule'. Stories of Kiely's stories. Stories of how he told stories. Stories of how his stories became songs. Songs, indeed, of his stories. No better music, and it's still sounding out.

There was absolutely no need for Ben to invite a young writer into his life, to tell him stories, to charge the world for him. But he did.

He opened the door in his pyjamas (he'd been writing since dawn), and later on that day we walked around Donnybrook together. It was an afternoon unlike any I had had before. It was split open with sunlight. There was a coin on the ground. I cannot remember its denomination, but I do recall Ben laughing and saying: 'Sometimes all that it takes to make a man happy is a ha'penny piece on the ground.' There were no ha'penny pieces left anymore in those days. Let's make it fifty pence and split it down the middle.

Like the after-image of a light that only by closing my eyes I can see, I recall the moment to be recalled again and again. I never met anyone like him before and had a fair idea that I would never meet anyone like him again. I went to his and Frances's house many times after that. It wouldn't be true to say he never changed. Of course he did. He grew older. His health began failing. The stories were slipping from him. The songs dipped away. No matter. He never died. Never will. The songs and words are still there. We will recognise them, always, as grace.

BENEDICT KIELY

•

A Select Bibliography

Counties of Contention: A Study of the Origins and Implications of the Partition of Ireland. Cork: Mercier, 1945; with an introduction by John Hume, 2004.

Land Without Stars. London: Christopher Johnson, 1946; Dublin: Moytura Press, 1990; with a 'Retrospect' by Benedict Kiely.

Poor Scholar: A Study of the Works and Days of William Carleton, 1794–1869. London: Sheed and Ward, 1947; Dublin: The Talbot Press, 1972.

In a Harbour Green. London: Jonathan Cape, 1949; New York: E.P. Dutton, 1950; Dublin: Moytura Press, 1992.

Modern Irish Fiction: A Critique. Dublin: Golden Eagle Books, 1950.

Call for a Miracle. London: Jonathan Cape, 1950; London: Catholic Book Club, n.d.; New York: E.P. Dutton, 1951.

Honey Seems Bitter. New York: E.P. Dutton, 1952; New York: Dell, 1952, as *The Evil that Men Do*; London: Methuen, 1954; Dublin: Moytura Press, 1992.

The Cards of the Gambler. London: Methuen, 1953; as *The Cards of the Gambler: A Folktale*; Dublin:

Millington, 1973; Dublin: Wolfhound Press, 1995, with an introduction by Thomas Flanagan; Dublin: New Island Books, 2010.

There was an Ancient House. London: Methuen, 1955; Dublin: Wolfhound Press, 1995.

The Captain with the Whiskers. London: Methuen, 1960; New York: Criterion Books, 1961; Dublin: Poolbeg Press, 1980; London: Methuen, 2004, with an afterword by Thomas Kilroy; London: Turnpike Books, 2016.

A Journey to the Seven Streams: Seventeen Stories. London: Methuen, 1963; Dublin: Poolbeg Press, 1977, as *A Journey to the Seven Streams and other stories*.

A Ball of Malt and Madame Butterfly: A Dozen Stories. London: Gollancz, 1973; Harmondsworth: Penguin, 1976.

Dogs Enjoy the Morning. London: Gollancz, 1968; Harmondsworth: Penguin: 1971; Dublin: Wolfhound Press, 1996; Dublin: New Island Books, 2017, with an introduction by Martina Devlin.

Proxopera. London: Gollancz, 1977; London/Dublin: Quartet Books/Poolbeg Press, 1979; London: Methuen, 1988; Boston: David Godine, 1986, with an afterword by the author. Also in *The State of Ireland: A Novella and Seventeen Stories*. Boston: David Godine, 1980; London: Penguin, 1982, with an introduction by Thomas Flanagan; *The Collected Stories of Benedict Kiely*: London: Methuen, 2001, with an introduction by Colum McCann; Boston: David Godine, 2003; London: Turnpike Books, 2015.

All the Way to Bantry Bay and other Irish Journeys. London: Gollancz, 1978.

A Cow in the House and nine other stories. London: Gollancz, 1978.

Dublin. Oxford: Oxford University Press, 1983.

Nothing Happens in Carmincross. London: Gollancz, 1985; Boston: David Godine, 1985.

The Aerofilms Book of Ireland from the Air. London: Weidenfeld and Nicolson, 1985.

A Letter to Peachtree and nine other stories. London: Gollancz, 1987; Boston: David Godine, 1988.

Yeats's Ireland: An Illustrated Anthology. London: Aurum, 1989; New York: Clarkson N. Potter, 1989 (as *Yeats's Ireland: An Enchanted Vision*), edited with an introduction by Benedict Kiely.

Drink to the Bird: Memoirs. London: Methuen, 1991.

God's Own Country: Selected Stories 1963–93. London: Minerva, 1993, with an introduction by the author.

'25 Views of Dublin' by James Horan. Commentary by Benedict Kiely. Essay by Peter Somerville-Large. Dublin: Town House, in association with the Office of Public Works, 1994.

And as I Rode by Granard Moat. Dublin: The Lilliput Press, 1996.

A Raid into Dark Corners and Other Essays. Cork: Cork University Press, 1999, with a preface by John Montague.

The Waves Behind Us: Further Memoirs. London: Methuen, 1999.

The Collected Stories of Benedict Kiely. London: Methuen, 2001, with an introduction by Colum McCann; Boston: David Godine, 2003.

Benedict Kiely: Selected Stories. Dublin: Liberties Press, 2011, edited with an afterword by Ben Forkner.

The Best of Benedict Kiely: A Selection of Short Stories. Dublin: New Island Books, 2019, with an introduction by Anthony Glavin.

Down then by Derry: Three Stories. London: Turnpike Books, 2019.

CONTRIBUTORS

Christopher Cahill, a native New Yorker, is the author of a novel, *Perfection* (1996), and a collection of poems, *The Drug of Choice* (2012). He is the editor of *There You Are: Writings on Irish and American Literature and History* by Thomas Flanagan (2004) and of *Gather 'Round Me: The Best of Irish Popular Poetry* (2004). Christopher Cahill serves as the Executive Director of the American Irish Historical Society, where for twenty years he edited *The Recorder*, the society's journal.

Paul Clements is a writer, broadcaster and journalist. The author of four discursive travel books about Ireland – including *Burren Country* (2011) and *Wandering Ireland's Wild Atlantic Way* (2016) – he is also a contributing writer to two guidebooks, *Fodor's Essential Ireland* and the *Rough Guide to Ireland*. His biography, *Romancing Ireland*, on the travel writer, actor and singer Richard Hayward, was adapted for BBC television. He has also written widely about the writer and historian Jan Morris. Paul Clements writes a regular local history book review column for *The Irish Times*.

Patricia Craig is a critic and author. Among her numerous books are *Brian Moore: A Biography* (2002) and

Bookworm: A Memoir of Childhood Reading (2015). She has edited many anthologies, including *The Oxford Book of Ireland* (1998), *The Belfast Anthology* (1999) and *The Ulster Anthology* (2006). She is a frequent contributor to *The Times Literary Supplement*, *The Irish Times* and the *Dublin Review of Books*, and has lectured and broadcast extensively. *Asking for Trouble*, the first volume of her trilogy of the same name, appeared in 2007, followed by *A Twisted Root: Ancestral Entanglements in Ireland* in 2012; and she is at present working on the third.

Gerald Dawe is a Belfast-born poet who has published over twenty books of poetry, including *Selected Poems* (2012) and *Mickey Finn's Air* (2014), as well as numerous volumes of literary essays, most recently *Of War and War's Alarms* (2015) and *The Wrong Country* (2018). He is Emeritus Professor of English and Fellow of Trinity College, Dublin. He lives in Dún Laoghaire.

Martina Devlin is an author and journalist. She has written ten books, from non-fiction to novels, including *About Sisterland* and *The House Where It Happened*. Her latest book is a short-story collection, *Truth and Dare: Short Stories about Women Who Changed Ireland*. Among the prizes she has received are the Royal Society of Literature's V.S. Pritchett Prize and a Hennessy Literary Award. She writes a weekly current affairs column for the *Irish Independent* and has been named National Newspapers of Ireland commentator of the year. Currently she is a doctoral candidate at Trinity College, Dublin.

Brian Fallon was born in County Cavan in 1933, the second son of the renowned poet Padraic Fallon. He is a former Literary Editor of *The Irish Times*, and was that newspaper's Art Critic for thirty-five years. He has written widely on the arts, and his numerous books include the critically significant surveys, *Irish Art 1830–1990* (1994) and *An Age of Innocence: Irish Culture 1930–1960* (1998). Fallon lives in County Wicklow with his wife Marion, a former journalist and broadcaster.

John Wilson Foster is Professor Emeritus at the University of British Columbia and honorary research professor at Queen's University, Belfast. Among his many books are *Forces and Themes in Ulster Fiction* (1974), *Fictions of the Irish Literary Revival: A Changeling Art* (1987) and *Irish Novels 1890–1940: New Bearings in Culture and Fiction* (2008). Other works include *Titanic* (1999). He has also published widely on natural history, including *Pilgrims of the Air: The Passing of the Passenger Pigeons* (2014).

Derek Hand is a Senior Lecturer and Head of the School of English at Dublin City University. He co-edited a special issue of the *Irish University Review* on Benedict Kiely in 2008. His numerous publications include *John Banville: Exploring Fictions* (2002) and *A History of the Irish Novel*, published by Cambridge University Press in 2011.

Thomas Kilroy, one of the leading Irish dramatists of his generation, has written eighteen plays for the stage, as well as a prize-winning novel, *The Big Chapel* (1971). In the 2004 *Irish Times* Theatre Awards he received a Special

Tribute; in 2008 he received the PEN Ireland Cross Award for Literature, and in 2016 the Ulysses Medal, awarded by University College Dublin. *Over the Backyard Wall: A Memory Book* was published in 2018.

Colum McCann is the author of six novels and three collections of short stories. He is co-founder of the global non-profit Narrative 4. Among the many awards his work has received are a National Book Award (US), the International Dublin IMPAC Prize and a Chevalier des Arts et Lettres from the French government. He is a member of Aosdána and the American Academy of the Arts. He lives in New York and teaches in the MFA programme at Hunter College. A new novel, *Apeirogon*, will be published in the spring of 2020.

George O'Brien has published an autobiographical trilogy – *The Village of Longing* (1987), *Dancehall Days* (1988) and *Out of Our Minds* (1994) – and various books of literary criticism, the most recent of which is *The Irish Novel 1800–1910* (2015). He is Professor Emeritus of English at Georgetown University, Washington DC.

Thomas O'Grady has been Director of the Irish Studies programme at the University of Massachusetts, Boston, since 1984. His critical essays on Irish literary and cultural matters have appeared widely, and he has written with particular expertise on the three major authors of south-east Ulster – William Carleton, Patrick Kavanagh and Benedict Kiely. A well-known poet, his second volume of poems, *Delivering the News*, was published in 2019.

ACKNOWLEDGMENTS

The editor wishes to express grateful thanks to the following: Frances Kiely, Jonathan Williams, Vincent Hurley, Máire Kennedy, Fiona Dunne, Myles McCionnaith and Pam O'Brien.

ENDNOTES

GEORGE O'BRIEN

1 Val Mulkerns, 'A Master Storyteller', *The Recorder: Journal of the American-Irish Historical Society* 7, i (Summer 1994), 44–51.

2 Derek Hand, 'Introduction: Benedict Kiely and the Persona of the Irish Writer', *Irish University Review* 38, i (Spring–Summer 2008; Special Benedict Kiely Number), vii–x (vii).

3 Thomas Kilroy, 'Afterword', *The Captain with the Whiskers* (London: Methuen, 2004), pp. 285–92 (285).

4 Benedict Kiely, *Modern Irish Fiction: A Critique* (Dublin: Golden Eagle Books, 1950), p. 67. It would not be Ben if then or later he allowed that view to be clouded by Clarke's rather lukewarm review of *Poor Scholar* (*The Times Literary Supplement*, 24 April 1948).

5 Thomas Flanagan, 'Benedict Kiely', in Christopher Cahill (ed.), *There You Are: Writings on Irish and American Literature and History [by Thomas Flanagan]* (New York: New York Review Books, 2004), p. 465.

6 Derek Hand, *A History of the Irish Novel* (Cambridge: Cambridge University Press, 2011), p. 212.

7 Liam de Paor, 'The Tyroneman', *The Recorder: Journal of the American-Irish Historical Society* 7, i (Summer 1994), 77–88.

8 For more on the O'Rathaille connection see 'Land without Stars: Aodhagán O'Rahilly' in Benedict Kiely, *A Raid into Dark Corners and Other Essays* (Cork: Cork University Press, 1999), pp. 8–30. This essay first appeared in the *Capuchin Annual* 1945–6, pp. 206–22.

9 Benedict Kiely, *Land Without Stars* ([London: Christopher Johnson, 1946]; Dublin: Moytura Press, 1990), pp. 14–15.

10   Benedict Kiely, 'A Sense of Place', in Seán Mac Réamoinn (ed.), *The Pleasures of Gaelic Poetry* (London: Allen Lane, 1982), pp. 93–109 (96).

11   de Paor, op. cit., p. 77.

12   Benedict Kiely, *Poor Scholar: A Study of the Work and Days of William Carleton (1794–1869)* ([London: Sheed and Ward, 1947]; Dublin: The Talbot Press, 1972), p. 140.

13   'Ned McKeown's Two Doors: An Approach to the Novel in Ireland', in *A Raid into Dark Corners*, p. 5. This essay first appeared in Tim Pat Coogan (ed.), *Ireland and the Arts* (London: Quartet, n.d. 'A special issue of *The Literary Review*').

14   *Poor Scholar*, p. 145.

15   This appreciation is most immediately available in the anthology-with-commentary, *Dublin* (Oxford: Oxford University Press, 1983), but it is also expressed in the introductory matter to, for instance, James Horan's *25 Views of Dublin* (Dublin: Town House in association with the Office of Public Works, 1994) and Bill Doyle's *Images of Dublin: A Time Remembered* (Dublin: The Lilliput Press, 2001).

16   The distinction is made both in *Dublin* (pp. 1–2) and in the memoir *The Waves Behind Us* (London: Methuen, 1999), p. 52. Ben's sense of the difference was no doubt deepened by his friendship with Brendan Behan, a literary and cultural connection meriting further study. See 'That Old Triangle: A Memory of Brendan Behan' in *A Raid into Dark Corners* (Cork: Cork University Press, 1999), pp. 169–80; originally in R.H.W. Dillard, George Garrett and John Rees Moore (eds), *The Sounder Few: Essays from* The Hollins Critic (Athens, Georgia: University of Georgia Press, 1971), pp. 85–99.

17   Three of Ben's novels were banned – *In a Harbour Green*, *Honey Seems Bitter* and *There was an Ancient House*. See 'The Whores on the Half-Doors, *Or* An Image of the Irish Writer', *The Kilkenny Magazine* 14 (Spring–Summer 1966); reprinted in Owen Dudley Edwards (ed.), *Conor Cruise O'Brien Introduces Ireland* (London: André Deutsch, 1969), pp. 148–61, and in *A*

Raid into Dark Corners, pp. 134–49; see also Julia Carlson, *Banned in Ireland* (Athens, Georgia: University of Georgia Press, 1990), pp. 21–35.

18   Thomas Flanagan, 'Introduction', *The Cards of the Gambler* (Dublin: Wolfhound Press, 1995), p. 7.

19   John Wilson Foster, 'Dogs Among the Moles: The Fictional World of Benedict Kiely', *The Dublin Magazine* (Series 3), 8, vi (1969), 24–65.

20   John Jordan, 'The Short Story after the Second World War', in Augustine Martin (ed.), *The Genius of Irish Prose* (Cork: Mercier Press, 1985), p. 134.

21   Elke D'Hoker, '"The Sound of a Man's Voice Speaking": Narrative Strategies in Benedict Kiely's Short Stories', *Irish University Review* 38, i (Spring–Summer 2008), 38–52.

22   Benedict Kiely, 'Afterword: A River at My Garden's End', *Proxopera: A Tale of Modern Ireland* (Boston: David Godine, 1986), pp. 95–117.

23   Seán Mac Réamoinn, 'A Seanchaí in the Authentic Tradition', *The Recorder: Journal of the American-Irish Historical Society* 7, i (Summer 1994), 100–2.

24   In addition to 'Land Without Stars', see also such pieces as 'Journey in Ulster', *Capuchin Annual* 1943, 495–501, and 'The House at Darrynane [*sic*]', *Capuchin Annual* 1946–7, 393–407.

25   Benedict Kiely, *All the Way to Bantry Bay and other Irish Journeys* (London: Gollancz, 1978), p. 172.

26   Benedict Kiely, *And as I Rode by Granard Moat* (Dublin: The Lilliput Press, 1996), p. 48.

27   Felix Kearney, 'The Hills above Drumquin', quoted in *And as I Rode by Granard Moat*, pp. 15–16.

28   See, for instance, 'Thanksgiving in the Hoosegow', *The Nation*, 25 November 1968, 553–7, and 'In the Week of Martin's Murder', in W.J. McCormack (ed.), *In the Prison of His Days* (Dublin: The Lilliput Press, 1988), pp. 50–5.

29   It should be noted, however, that visiting America did not inspire Ben's devotion to the short story. He was already contributing to the *New Yorker* before going there. His first

work in the form to be published there was 'The White Wild Bronco', which appeared in the 20 December 1958 issue.

30 *All the Way to Bantry Bay*, p. 19.

BRIAN FALLON

1 There are, in fact, signs that things already are changing, though slowly. In Dublin, personal factors often tend to be strong when it comes to assessing or reassessing a writer's reputation.

2 Wescott – unnamed, but recognisable – is caricatured in Hemingway's *The Sun Also Rises* as one of a group of Paris-based homosexuals hanging around Lady Brett Ashley, the English aristocrat loved by Jake Barnes, the narrator.

3 See Kiely's essay, 'Love & Pain & Parting: The Novels of Kate O'Brien' in *A Raid into Dark Corners and Other Essays* (Cork: Cork University Press, 1999), pp. 55–65.

4 See his Foreword to Stephen Haddelsey, *Charles Lever: The Lost Victorian* (Gerrards Cross: Colin Smythe, 2000).

5 References to the French and Russian masters recur most frequently in Kiely's criticism and literary allusions, with references to German literature very much less frequent. However, Donagh Hartigan, the protagonist of *Honey Seems Bitter*, is a reader of Rilke and Kafka.

MARTINA DEVLIN

1 Julia Carlson, *Banned in Ireland: Censorship and the Irish Writer* (London: Routledge, 1990), p. 31.

GERALD DAWE

1 NUU was established, amidst controversy, outside Coleraine in 1968. Many were of the opinion that it should have been located in Derry/Londonderry where Magee College already had long-established academic and cultural ties to Trinity College, Dublin. Now known as Ulster University, it is the largest university in Northern Ireland.

2 See David McKittrick, Seamus Kelters, Brian Feeney, Chris Thornton and David McVea, *Lost Lives: The Stories of the Men, Women and Children Who Died as a Result of the Northern Irish Conflict* (Edinburgh: Mainstream Publishing, 2007), p. 1494.

3 Anthony Cronin, 'The Dark Side of Carleton', *The Irish Times*, 5 April 1974.

4 Thomas Flanagan, *The Irish Novelists 1800–1850* (New York: Columbia University Press, 1959).

5 William Carleton, *The Autobiography of William Carleton*, with a Preface by Patrick Kavanagh (London: MacGibbon and Kee, 1968).

6 William Carleton, *Stories from Carleton*, with an Introduction by W.B. Yeats (London: Walter Scott, 1889).

7 The quotations that follow are taken from this edition of *Poor Scholar*. Sheed and Ward was a publishing house founded in London in 1926 by Catholic activists Frank Sheed and Maisie Ward. The house published a number of Catholic literary figures during the mid-twentieth century.

8 Sesquipidalian: characterised by long words, long-winded. Derived from the mid-seventeenth century and the Latin *sesquipidalis*, 'a foot and a half long'.

9 James Plunkett, *Strumpet City* (London: Hutchinson, 1969).

10 Arthur Koestler, *Darkness at Noon* (London: Macmillan, 1940).

11 Benedict Kiely, *Counties of Contention: A Study of the Origins and Implications of the Partition of Ireland* (Cork: Mercier Press, 1945; with an introduction by John Hume, 2004).

12 Benedict Kiely, *Modern Irish Fiction: A Critique* (Dublin: Golden Eagle Books, 1950).

DEREK HAND

1 Benedict Kiely, *Modern Irish Fiction: A Critique* (Dublin: Golden Eagle, 1950), p. vi.

2 See Declan Kiberd, *Inventing Ireland: The Literature of the Modern Nation* (London: Jonathan Cape, 1995), p. 263ff.

3   Seamus Deane, 'Introduction', Edward Said, et al., *Nationalism, Colonialism, Literature* (Minneapolis: University of Minnesota Press, 1990), p. 13.

4   Seán O'Faoláin, 'Ah, Wisha! The Irish Novel', *Virginia Quarterly Review* 17, ii (Spring 1941), 265–74.

5   Kiely, *Modern Irish Fiction*, p. vi.

6   See, for instance, Brian Fallon, *An Age of Innocence: Irish Culture 1930–1960* (Dublin: Gill and Macmillan, 1998) and Gerald Dawe, *The Wrong Country: Essays on Modern Irish Writing* (Dublin: Irish Academic Press, 2018).

7   An early reviewer of *The Cards of the Gambler* recognised that it was 'a novel of modern life'. See 'A New Novel: *The Cards of the Gambler*', *Irish Independent*, 24 January 1953.

8   Brian Friel, *The Irish Monthly* 81, cmlviii (June 1953), 249–50.

9   Walter Benjamin, *The Arcades Project* (Cambridge, Massachusetts: The Belknap Press of Harvard University Press, 2002), p. 510.

10 *Ibid.*, p. 510ff.

11 'A New Novel: *The Cards of the Gambler*', *Irish Independent*, 24 January 1953.

12 Grace Eckley, *Benedict Kiely* (New York: Twayne, 1972), p. 113.

13 'We make out of the quarrel with others, rhetoric, but of the quarrel with ourselves, poetry', W.B. Yeats, *Per Amica Silentia Lunæ* (New York: Macmillan, 1918), p. 30.

14 Eckley, *op. cit.*, p. 114.

15 James Joyce, *Ulysses*. Edited with an Introduction by Declan Kiberd (Harmondsworth: Penguin, 1992), p. 42.

16 T.S. Eliot, 'The Waste Land', in Margaret Ferguson, Mary Jo Salter and Jon Stallworthy (eds), *The Norton Anthology of Poetry* (New York: Norton, 1996. 4th Edition), p. 1248.

17 Kiely, *Modern Irish Fiction*, p. viii.

18 Fallon, *op. cit.*, p. 271.

JOHN WILSON FOSTER

1   E.M. Forster, *Aspects of the Novel* (London: Arnold, 1927), p. 21.

2 See Eliot, 'Tradition and the Individual Talent' in, for instance, Frank Kermode (ed.), *Selected Prose of T.S. Eliot* (London: Faber, 1975), pp. 37–44. For reasons I will leave unexamined, this notion of tradition may be more congenial to an Irish rather than an English writer. My associating Ben with Forster and Eliot in this regard is justified by the enormous range of literary reference and allusion in his short stories, novels, memoirs and criticism, and it satisfies Eliot's call for a European literary awareness.

3 Although the traditional song was one of Ben's favourite oral genres, it was unnecessary for the song to be venerable. One line of Ian and Sylvia's 'Four Strong Winds' is quoted by a character in the story 'Secondary Top' (*A Letter to Peachtree*, 1987), and another by the narrator. Towards the end of 'A Letter to Peachtree', the narrator silently quotes the unidentified 1940s' ballad 'I'll Walk Alone'. I recall a later, pre-Google disagreement we had about whether a late-1950s rock singer we both had liked, Billy Fury, was still alive. Incidentally, Ben's pleasure in the demotic separated him from his beloved Yeats. In his soft spot for certain examples of sentimental popular art, he resembled Joyce.

4 Despite his endless anecdotes, Ben had little of what we call small talk, or concern for the domestic, any more than apparently Yeats did. After the initial greeting and during the welcoming glass, his talk instantly entered performance – chiefly monologue and recitation – but in no affected or stagey way; he simply and naturally raised the bar of conversation.

5 Yeats, of course, was in literature his chief of men, and Ben could quote him till the cattle returned, and did. His sonorous and unmistakable voice (loyal listeners to RTÉ's *Sunday Miscellany* delighted in putting a face to the radio voice when they overheard it in restaurants) was a more fitting instrument for Yeats's reflectively inquiring middle poems than the poet's own higher-pitched voice. Ben could not but be aware of the resonance of his voice and was even willing to spoof it, as he does in 'A Letter to Peachtree,' in which the character Patrick Lagan (Kiely's

pseudonym when he wrote his *Irish Press* column on travel and local history) is 'a helluva man to quote poetry. In a booming base barreltone that would put Ariel to sleep.' This portmanteau coinage 'base barreltone' is silently borrowed from the description of Ben Dollard's voice in *Ulysses* and is re-borrowed in 'There are Meadows in Lanark', where it becomes 'bass barreltone'.

6   Edward Arlington Robinson, *Collected Poems* (New York: Macmillan, 1922), p. 573.

7   'The Uncle. A Mystery', in Henry Glassford Bell, *Summer and Winter Hours* (Edinburgh: Constable; London: Hurst, Chance, 1831). Kiely transposes one verse and if there are a couple of small errors, it may be because he is quoting a poem that he has learned by heart. On the other hand, the narrator gives a physical description of the book which tallies with the 1890s Glasgow edition, so it may well have been in Kiely's possession.

8   *With Appendix: A Study of the Poem*. Glasgow, *c*.1897. 'The Uncle' was a popular performance piece, and the narrator tells us that even 'Sir Henry Irving' recited it to music.

9   Earlier, in the title story to Kiely's first collection, *A Journey to the Seven Streams* (1963), television dooms the crossroads dancing and minstrelsy.

10   The Eton Crop was in vogue in the 1920s but came later, no doubt, to rural Ireland. In lieu of Anna, Eugene keeps a picture of Ginger Rogers underneath the lid of his school desk. He would have seen Rogers at the cinema in the 1930s, the decade of her greatest popularity.

11   The central character tallies during a hangover the loss of friends in death and changing mores, which echoes such disappearing Dublin landmarks as the Scotch House pub and the Red Bank restaurant. Like Farrington in Joyce's 'Counterparts', Ben patronised the Scotch House before it was replaced by offices in the 1980s, when the story is probably set, though 'Bloodless Byrne' would not be entirely out of place in *Dubliners*. The Red Bank was also a Kiely haunt. It closed in 1969. During the Second World War it had a reputation as a resort for Dublin's German Nazi colony.

CHRISTOPHER CAHILL

1 Drawing on memory, perhaps, Ben slightly misquotes. What de Valera said was: 'The ideal Ireland that we would have, the Ireland that we dreamed of, would be the home of a people who were satisfied with material wealth only as a basis for right living, of a people who were satisfied with frugal comfort and devoted their leisure to things of the spirit – a land whose countryside would be bright with cosy homesteads, whose fields and villages would be joyous with the sounds of industry, with the romping of sturdy children, the contests of athletic youths and the laughter of happy maidens, whose firesides would be forums for the wisdom of serene old age. The home, in short, of a people living the life that God desires that men should live.' (https://www.rte.ie/archives/exhibitions/eamon-de-valera/719124-address-by-mr-de-valera/) But this also differs from the address as reproduced in Maurice Moynihan (ed.), *Speeches and Statements of Eamon de Valera* (Dublin: Gill and Macmillan, 1980), pp. 466–9. See letter from John Bowman, *The Irish Times*, 14 June 2004.

2 Benedict Kiely, *All the Way to Bantry Bay* (London: Gollancz, 1978), p. 163.

3 Citations to 'Letters from America' are from copies in the author's collection. This material is included in the Benedict Kiely Papers at the National Library of Ireland, V. ii. 18–20.

4 'The Dogs in the Great Glen' was first published in *The New Yorker*, 8 October 1960.

5 George Steiner, *After Babel: Aspects of Language and Translation* (New York: Oxford University Press, 1975), p. 184.

6 Hugo von Hofmannsthal, *The Lord Chandos Letter and Other Writings* (New York: New York Review Books, 2005), p. 124.

7 Harry Mathews, *Cigarettes* (New York: Weidenfeld and Nicolson, 1987), p. 291.

THOMAS O'GRADY

1   Benedict Kiely, *Proxopera: A Novel* (London: Gollancz, 1977), p. 64. Subsequent quotations from this edition will be noted parenthetically in the body of the essay.

2   E.M. Forster, *Aspects of the Novel* (New York: Harcourt Brace Jovanovich, 1955), p. 86.

3   Benedict Kiely, 'Afterword: A River at My Garden's End', *Proxopera: A Tale of Modern Ireland* (Boston: David Godine, 1986), p. 95.

4   Benedict Kiely, *Drink to the Bird* (London: Methuen, 1991), p. 147.

5   'A River at My Garden's End', p. 98.

6   See Frank McCrory, 'The Treacherous Waves of Lough Muck' in Benedict Kiely, *And as I Rode by Granard Moat* (Dublin: Lilliput, 1996), pp. 29–31.

7   See Richard Ellmann, *Ulysses on the Liffey* (Oxford: Oxford University Press, 1972), p. 188.

8   James Joyce, *Ulysses* (New York: Vintage, 1986), p. 31.

9   Don Gifford and Robert J. Seidman, Ulysses *Annotated: Notes for James Joyce's* Ulysses (Berkeley, California: University of California Press, 1988), p. 45.

10 For a detailed description of this tradition, see Whitley Stokes, 'The Prose Tales in the Rennes Dindsenchas', *Revue Celtique* XV (1894), 272–336, 418–84. Stokes summarises the tradition as 'a collection of stories (*senchasa*), in Middle-Irish prose and verse, about the names of noteworthy places (*dind*) in Ireland – plains, mountains, ridges, cairns, lakes, rivers, fords, estuaries, islands, and so forth' (272).

11 Joyce, letter to Carlo Linati, 21 September 1920, in Richard Ellmann (ed.), *Selected Letters of James Joyce* (London: Faber, 1975), p. 271.

12 Jay David Bolter, *Writing Space: The Computer, Hypertext, and the History of Writing* (Hillsdale, NY: Erlbaum, 1991), p. 24.

13 Michael Groden, 'Introduction to "James Joyce's *Ulysses* in Hypermedia"', *Journal of Modern Literature* XXIV, 3–4 (Summer 2001), 359–62.

14 George P. Landow, *Hypertext: The Convergence of Contemporary Critical Theory and Technology* (Baltimore: Johns Hopkins University Press, 1992), p. 10.

15 Robert Rhodes James (ed.), *Winston S. Churchill: His Complete Speeches 1897–1963* (New York: Chelsea House, 1974), Vol. VI, p. 6238.

16 James Joyce, *Ulysses* (New York: Vintage, 1986), p. 28.